BEREAVEMENT AND SUPPORT

BEREAVEMENT AND SUPPORT
Healing in a Group Environment

Marylou Hughes, L.C.S.W., D.P.A.
Private Practice
Fort Pierce, Florida

Taylor & Francis
Publishers since 1798

USA	Publishing Office:	TAYLOR & FRANCIS 325 Chestnut Street Philadelphia, PA 19106 Tel: (215) 625-8900 Fax: (215) 625-2940
	Distribution Center:	TAYLOR & FRANCIS 7625 Empire Drive Florence, KY 41042 Tel: 800-634-7064 Fax: 800-248-4724
UK		TAYLOR & FRANCIS LTD. 27 Church Road Hove E. Sussex, BN3 2FA Tel: +44 (0) 1273 207411 Fax: +44 (0) 1273 205612

BEREAVEMENT AND SUPPORT: Healing in a Group Environment

4   5   6   7   8   9   0   BRBR   9   8   7

This book was set in Times Roman by Harlowe Typography, Inc. The editors were Nancy Geltman and Holly Seltzer. Prepress supervisor was Miriam Gonzalez. Cover design by Michelle Fleitz. Printing and binding by Braun-Brumfield, Inc.

A CIP catalog record for this book is available from the British Library.
⊗ The paper in this publication meets the requirements of the ANSI Standard Z39.48-1984 (Permanence of Paper)

Library of Congress Cataloging-in-Publication Data
Hughes, Marylou.
    Bereavement and support: healing in a group environment/Marylou Hughes.
        p. cm. — (Series in death education, aging and health care)
    Includes bibliographical references.

    1. Bereavement—Psychological aspects. 2. Grief. 3. Death—Psychological aspects.
4. Group counseling. 5. Self-help groups.
I. Title. II. Series.
BF575.G7H84   1995
155.9′37—dc20
                                                                                94-43544
                                                                                CIP

ISBN 1-56032-370-1 (case)
ISBN 1-56032-371-X (paper)
ISSN 0275-3510

Dedicated to Lilian McIlroy

Contents

Preface

Twenty years ago bereavement support groups were all but unheard of. Now they are sponsored by funeral homes, volunteer organizations, hospices, hospitals, churches, nursing homes, senior citizen organizations, psychotherapists in private practice, employee assistance programs, self-help groups, schools, social service agencies, and any number of associations that have been founded to meet the needs of specific populations of bereaved people.

Not all the bereaved want or need group support. Those who find a group that meets their needs become true believers in the group process, benefit from their experience, and pass the word to others who may also profit from participation in a bereavement support group.

Bereavement support groups are a form of magic. They are made up of an assortment of unrelated people who have only their loss and pain in common. An alchemy takes place, and the individuals develop close emotional bonds. The mutual support and understanding helps them emerge from the group in a more positive state of mind.

Bereavement groups have become so popular that many people are being called upon to organize and facilitate groups. People who have survived their own experience of loss and have professional back-up or training are sought to facilitate bereavement support groups. They emotionally and intellectually understand that the major source of help for each group member is the other group members who share in their struggle.

In this book the support group leader will find information on how to organize and start a bereavement support group, how to keep the group going, and how to bring the group to a close. It differs from other group work books in that theory and practice are melded into a how-to approach. No one method or form is recommended over another. The many possibilities are presented for consideration and choice.

This book will give the neophyte group leader confidence and will confirm the knowledge of the seasoned group leader. Everyone who reads this book will gain ideas and understanding.

I would like to acknowledge Carol Pendleton, Hospice staff members and volunteers, Ruth J. L. Richard, Anne Studner, and Widowed Persons Service staff and volunteers.

Marylou Hughes

Chapter 1

A Theoretical Overview

According to Ariés's (1981) research, attitudes toward death prevail for thousands of years, shifting only slowly as historical events and emerging beliefs affect practices. Indifference in ancient times was followed by emotional reactions to death, which persisted until the seventeenth century, when the prevailing culture mandated that emotional displays be controlled. Early recorded history documents that a presentiment about one's own death was expected, documented, and believed. In the thirteenth century unusual and untimely deaths were frightening and thus not talked about.

Ariés explains that rituals of mourning came out of the Middle Ages, with the ritual eventually being simplified by the practice of religious modesty.

Ariés reports that in the 1800s death was seen as peaceful and pleasant. Early American settlers were expected to be brave, stoic, and accepting in death.

Ariés observes that present death customs in the Western world emphasize denial. Mourning customs are no longer observed, and there is no perceptible pause to mark the death of a person. Life goes on as it has been.

Ariés notes that efforts to deny death are not working. Death as a loss to be acknowledged is in the forefront.

ATTITUDES ABOUT DEATH

Death is the unacceptable alternative. Loved ones are expected to fight death, be good patients, do what has to be done to survive, follow the physicians' advice, and get well. In the American culture it is possible for people to deceive themselves about the inevitability of death because people are living longer, machines keep patients alive in segregated sections of hospitals, youthful life-styles have become the established norm, and loss of vigor and self-control is derided (Stoddard, 1978). Dying is evidence of failure (Thomas, 1980). Thomas intones that Americans have not lost their fear of dying, but their respect for it. In 1978 Ross and Duff found that passive euthanasia was favored by 98% of the pediatricians that they studied in the New Haven area. Active euthanasia was approved by 39% of the pediatricians polled, and 33% opposed it. Mixed feelings were expressed by 28% of this group of physicians.

In 1961 Oken learned that 9% of 219 staff members of the Michael Reese Hospital in Chicago never told patients of their impending deaths. Another 47% very rarely told, and 29% occasionally did. Only 3% often explained the prognosis to the patients. A 1979 study reflects the change in how physicians see their responsibilities to dying patients (Novack). The researchers found that 98% of the doctors they questioned favored telling cancer patients when they were terminally ill. Only 2% of the respondents said that they made frequent exceptions to the policy of telling.

These attitudes about death influence how friends and relatives of the deceased manage their mourning. Hope and miracles are pursued. Although there is more awareness of death, survivors continue to think they could have done something to forestall the death. Even though the dying are frequently urged to talk about their journey, they are expected to remain cheerful and involved with life. This dichotomy is carried over into the mourning process. There is no set ritual. Grieving family members are exhorted to mourn, but not for too long. Expressions of deep mourning such as wearing black, staying at home for an extended period, and refraining from frivolous activities are discouraged. Dying and funeral patterns are in disarray. I have heard many stories that show this progression: People remember family members sitting at the bedsides of their grandparents until they died. But their parents died alone in hospitals. Friends who died recently were cremated without any ceremony or means of paying respects. If there is a funeral, black mourning attire is seldom seen. At most, businesses grant members of the immediate family three days of excused leave. The message is that life goes on and work comes first. Yet mourners frequently cannot comply with society's expectation of what grief should be.

GRIEF DEFINED

Worden (1991) defines grief as a normal reaction to loss and mourning as the process that the grieving person experiences. Bereavement is the adaptation to the loss. The Department of Health and Human Services (1981) refers to grief as a continuing, natural, and individual reaction to loss, whereas mourning is seen as the cultural response to grief. Bereavement is the state of having suffered a loss.

THE STUDY OF GRIEF

Grief as a normal reaction to loss was identified and written about as early as 1917. Sigmund Freud said that mourning was not pathological; it would be overcome after a time, and interfering with it was useless and probably harmful. In 1940 Melanie Klein wrote *Mourning and Its Relation to Manic-Depressive States,* in which she suggested that the mourner goes through a transitory manic-depressive state and overcomes it. In 1944 Lindemann claimed that "acute grief would not seem to be a medical or psychiatric disorder . . . but . . . a normal reaction to a distressing situation" (pp. 141–148). He went on to describe the symptoms of normal grief as "waves" of physical distress "lasting from twenty minutes to an hour," "tightness in the throat, choking," "shortness of breath," "sighing," "an empty feeling in the stomach," weakness, "tension," and poor appetite. Additionally there is a feeling of "unreality," withdrawal from others, "preoccupation with the image of the deceased," thoughts of negligence and "guilt," anger, "restlessness," pressure of speech, and an inability to "initiate and maintain organized patterns of activity." Lindemann said that the length of the grief reaction depended on the person's success in completing the grief "work." He and other researchers have described the overall effects of grief on the lives of the bereaved, the consequences of loss for the physical, social, emotional, behavioral, and intellectual functioning of the bereaved.

Marris (1958) studied widows in London, England. He found many of the same symptoms that Lindemann did but also commented on the widows' inability to acknowledge their loss. They brooded over their memories, clung to possessions, felt the presence of the deceased, and talked to them.

In 1965 Gorer reported that among the 80 bereaved he studied, 15 said that they never forget and never get over the loss.

Parkes (1972) calls grief the price paid for love. Grief and joy are both part of life. If people ignore that truth, then they will be unprepared for life's losses. Parkes likens a loss to a physical injury. It is a blow; a wound occurs, and there is healing. When complications or other injuries occur, healing does not take place or is retarded. Tatelbaum (1989, p. xiii) also uses the metaphor of a wound and suggests "tools" for healing in her book *You Don't Have to Suffer.*

In Lopata's 1973 study of widows, 48% of the participants told her that they were over their husbands' deaths in a year's time. But 20% said that they were not over their husband's death and did not expect ever to get over it.

A 1974 study (Glick, Weiss, and Parkes) revealed that men and women react differently to being bereaved. In that study, the men felt that they had lost part of themselves, but the women felt abandoned. Although the men accepted the death more rapidly, they were uncomfortable expressing grief and found it harder to work during their bereavement than did the women.

Loneliness, a common complaint of widows and widowers, appears to differ among widows in urban and rural locations. Kunkel (cited in Atchley, 1988) found that only a fourth of a sample of widows in small towns had problems with loneliness. Lopata (1973) and Blau (1961) found much greater loneliness among urban widows. Atchley's (1975) study revealed no difference in loneliness reported by older widows and widowers.

Berardo (1968, 1970) believes widowers have more difficulty adjusting than widows because men are unaccustomed to taking care of a household and of themselves. However, Bell (1971) concluded that older widows have more problems than older widowers because women encounter more financial hardships, have fewer opportunities to remarry, and lose the role of being a wife, which is more important to them than being a husband is for men. They become more socially isolated. In Atchley's (1975) comparison of widows and widowers, aged 70 to 79, he found more anxiety among widows, while the widowers suffered more from alienation, normlessness, and powerlessness. Widowers were more active socially, especially in the case of the working class. Atchley decided that working-class widows were less socially active than widowers because of inadequate income, which lowered their social participation and increased their loneliness.

Kunkel (cited in Atchley, 1988) compared widows and widowers over age 50 who lived in a small town. She found that although widowers had less interaction with their families and friends than did widows, they were satisfied. Widows had more interaction, but they were not satisfied and wanted more.

In 1981 Susser reviewed 14 studies spanning the years 1858 to 1981, which indicated that widowed men die more readily after the death of their spouse than do women. In the first 6 months after the deaths of their wives, men die at a rate exceeding that of married and remarried men. That mortality was still observable in a follow-up three years later. Susser questions whether these results should be attributed to the distress caused by the loss itself or to the stress of bereavement caused by the environmental situation.

When researchers separate the widows and widowers who gave long-term care to sick spouses from those whose spouses died suddenly, a different picture emerges. Smith (cited in Traub, 1990) studied 5,000 married couples from 1968 through 1989 and found that 13% of the men and 49% of the women who cared for their deceased spouses through a prolonged illness were more likely to die than the non-widowed.

Wolfelt (1990) sees men's grief as naturally complicated because of difficulty in overcoming their social conditioning to repress their feelings; they need to appear self-sufficient, cannot let themselves appear nonproductive, and cannot ask for help.

In 1989 Zisook (cited in Ritter, 1989) reported on a study of 300 widowed people and determined that those aged 56 and older did better than those aged 55 and younger. Older widowed people suffered less depression and anxiety 7 months after the death of the spouse than did the younger widowed.

Bereavement is different for men and women, and also for parents of deceased children. Sanders (1979–1980) interviewed 109 individuals who had relatives who had died. She found that bereaved parents experienced more intense grief, a wider range of reactions, and greater emotional and physical distress than people whose parents or spouses had died. Rando (1985) reviewed that study and others and concluded that the "unique factors of parental bereavement" (pp. 19–23) contribute to their profound grief. These parents experience survival guilt, a threat to their immortality, loss of hopes and dreams for the child, loss of the child's love, and loss of the parental role. They are often unable to support each other because of their individual grief and grieving styles and are reminded through a lifetime that the deceased child is not alive to achieve any of the normal milestones. Other parents may find their loss so upsetting that they do not know what to say or do and end up avoiding them.

In 1986 Knapp studied parents' reaction to the death of a child. He talked with 150 families and found common themes. The agony over the death of a child endures, as do the memories, which the parents do not want to relinquish. They wish for their own death. They search for meaning and become more tolerant, focus more on the family, and often turn to religion as they look for a reason for survival.

In 1985 Obershaw spoke to the Widowed Persons Service conference on the myths about grieving. He debunked the myths, saying that grief is not something a person gets over. People get through it, and do so by working at it, not by waiting for time to heal them. That they suffer the pain of grief does not mean that the bereaved have lost their faith; it means that they have experienced a traumatic loss. He does not believe in anticipatory grief, nor does he think individuals go through demarcated stages of grief. There is no steady forward movement. There are setbacks, up and downs, and always new challenges. Obershaw thus sees loss and grief not as despair, but as an opportunity for new experiences and growth.

When Silverman wrote *Helping Women Cope With Grief* (1981), she indicated that people know who they are by the way others treat them. When there is the loss of an important relationship, disorganization occurs. The bereaved need to develop new identities based on changed responsibilities, interests, and directions in their lives.

Children are not immune to the suffering of bereavement. Because of their dependence on adults for care, communication, and understanding, they may have more problems with loss than do adults. Loss that is realized and integrated at one age rears up and needs to be worked through at another age. As children go through developmental stages, their mentality changes. What was settled at age 3 needs to be revisited at age 13.

In 1985 Sandra Fox spoke on children's understanding of death, explaining that children through the age of 5 do not conceptualize death. They think the dead are still alive but living in a different dimension. They wonder how the deceased manage to go about their activities of daily living in their changed circumstances.

By the time children reach the age of 6, they understand that death is not reversible and struggle to understand it. They wonder who dies, why they die, and what happens to them.

Children aged 9 to 12 have an intellectual understanding that no one escapes death. They want to be involved in tangible death rituals, such as the funeral.

Adolescents are outraged by death. They are dramatic in their sorrow or embarrassed by the occurrence of a death. They are able to grieve openly with their friends over the death of a friend, but feel different and set apart from their friends when there is a death in their family.

Kastenbaum's (1967) explanation of children's reactions to death is similar to Fox's. Nagy (1948) studied children aged 3 to 10 and agrees with these developmental delineations. She posits that children's main questions are, "What is death?" "What makes people die?" and "What happens to people when they die; where do they go?" (p. 327).

Bowlby (1980), Furman (1964), and Freud and Burlingham (1942) wrote about their observations of grief in very young children. Furman points out children's differences in ability to comprehend death. Some 2-year-olds can understand what some 5-year-olds cannot. Bowlby and Freud and Burlingham have documented grieving observed in infants.

In validating the effects of early loss at later stages of development, Brown (1982) wrote that the death of a child's mother leads to clinical depression later in life. Silverman (1987) found that college-aged women continued to be tearful and have trouble talking about the death of a parent years after it occurred.

Researchers and practitioners agree that children should be told about death, allowed to participate in the rituals related to the death, be given time to mourn in their own way, and helped to feel secure in their living situation.

PHASES OF GRIEF

Many researchers who have studied the symptoms of grief believe that the bereaved go through identifiable phases on their struggle toward a life-style that incorporates memories of the deceased and adjustment to their absence. The number of phases ranges from Pollock's (1961) two to Westberg's (1973) ten. In 1961 Engel designated six phases, which he labeled shock and disbelief, developing awareness, restitution, resolving the loss, idealization, and the outcome. The idea of phases took hold when Kubler-Ross popularized the five phases of dying in 1969. The phases of denial (this can't happen to me), bargaining (give me one more chance and I will never tell another lie), anger (life is unfair), depression (it is hopeless), and acceptance (peace and readiness to move on) have also been applied to grief. Parkes (1972) identified four phases, which he called numbness, searching and pining, depression, and recovery. O'Connor (1984) wrote of stages of grief that incorporate the tasks of the bereaved: breaking old habits, beginning to reconstruct life, seeking new love objects and friends, and readjustment completed.

Briese and Farra (1984) proposed that grief theory based on phases is misleading, that no one goes through the phases sequentially, and that the ideal stage of acceptance or recovery is unrealistic and unhelpful. They suggested an alternative way of viewing the grief process that they believed was more acceptable to men. Instead of a method based primarily on emotion, they proposed a model based on life components, namely, self, others, work, community, and transcendence. Depending on the stresses, responsibilities, and priorities of life, a person invests more or less energy into each of the areas. There is no progression, however. One phase does not have to be accomplished to realize another. Rather it is a matter of where one's life energy is directed at different periods.

Sanders's (1989) phases of grief incorporate shock, awareness, conservation, and the turning point, and end with renewal. Neeld (1990) talks about life as it was, the process of change, and life back in balance. Through this course she weaves seven choices that involve accepting both despair and relief, what is missed and what is not missed, experiencing the feelings of grief, observing what is happening, and deciding to do something about it. Life gets better when the bereaved embody change, look ahead instead of back, tackle problems, re-examine themselves, and achieve their own transformation. The last phase, integration, occurs when the bereaved become comfortable with who they have become and find that they can make choices based on what they have learned.

In all the phases of grief, thoughts, feelings, physical responses, social relationships, and coping techniques are affected. The Grief Education Institute (Spangler, 1988) identifies the shock stage as a time of passive numbness. That is followed by protest, with physical and emotional anguish, and disorganization characterized by painful drifting, lack of interest, and loneliness. The last stage, reorganization, is accomplished when there is a reawakening to life, a return of physical and emotional health, and a renewal of relationships, when coping skills are once again effective.

Anyone having a personal acquaintance with loss and bereavement will disagree with any distinct delineation of symptoms, and so does the Grief Education Institute. Its publication on bereavement support groups carries the statement that, "categories are not . . . sharp and distinct. Stages . . . and manifestations vary greatly among individuals" (Spangler, 1988, p. 69). Worden (1986), in fact, states that the bereaved do not go through any particular stages, but instead have certain tasks that need to be accomplished.

Anyone who experiences loss suffers symptoms of grief. Adult grief has been studied at length, but the grief of children has not been neglected.

Phases of grief have been recognized in infants and young children. In 1960 Bowlby wrote about the three phases of mourning in infancy and early childhood. In Phase 1 the focus is on the missing person. Because that person is no longer there, there is disappointment, angry efforts to recover the lost person, and separation anxiety. Phase 2 is accomplished if the grieving child ceases to focus on the missing loved one. In Phase 3 the work of mourning is completed, and reorganization leads to a new and different state.

TASKS OF GRIEF

E. Lindemann identified the course of normal grief in 1944, calling it "grief work." The duration of the grief, according to him, depends on the success of the grief work, which results in "emancipation from the bondage to the deceased, readjustment to the environment in which the deceased is missing and the formation of new relationships" (pp. 141-148). In a speech in 1993, Worden added a task: "To experience the pain of grief."

Shuchter's (1986) tasks, which are similar to Lindemann's and Worden's, comprise living with the pain, continuing a relationship with the deceased, taking care of the self, developing other relationships, and becoming a healthy, confident person with a balanced view of the world.

These tasks take the bereaved from finding the most adaptive way to get through the pain, to emotionally separating from the deceased, to setting new goals, and developing a set of beliefs that fit the evolved life-style. Shuchter compares the last task to the adolescent's struggle for identity.

Wolfelt (1988) calls his five tasks the reconciliation needs of mourning. They are similar to Lindemann's, Shuchter's, and Worden's. His fifth reconciliation is significant enough to add to the tasks already listed: "To relate the experience of loss to a context of meaning." Rando (1992) also acknowledged the necessity of these tasks, labeling them the six *R* processes of recognizing the loss, reacting to the separation, recollecting the deceased and re-experiencing feelings, relinquishing old attachments to the deceased, readjusting in the new world without forgetting the old, and reinvesting in ways that realize gratification in other ways.

Fox (1985) spoke of the tasks of bereaved children, explaining that it is crucial that they know that the deceased loved ones will never been seen again. Children must be encouraged to experience and express their feelings, be given the opportunity to commemorate the lives of the loved ones, and be helped to get back to their normal routine. When there is an early death of the mother, it is necessary for loss to lead to transformation, and sadness to hope (Cole, 1992).

COMPLICATED GRIEF

Wolfelt (1988) and Worden (1993) differentiate between normal grief and clinical depression. In depression there is low self-esteem. In grief there may be lack of self-confidence, but the bereaved do not see life as a failure, think that they are not as good as others, or think people dislike them and are unfriendly.

People experiencing normal grief respond to comfort and support; clinically depressed people do not accept support, are irritable and complain, but are not usually openly angry. Those in grief can more readily express their anger.

The bereaved know why they are depressed. The depressed do not know what caused the depression. The depressed know no joy. The bereaved can experience moments of pleasure. Both the depressed and bereaved exhibit feelings of sadness and emptiness, but the clinically depressed also project hopelessness.

The bereaved may have flare-ups of chronic physical complaints. People with depression have many and constant physical complaints. The bereaved may have guilt feelings over some aspect of the deceased's death. People with clinical depression have overall feelings of guilt.

The bereaved may feel depressed and have symptoms of depression such as anxiety, problems with eating and sleeping, withdrawal, feelings that they want to die, poor concentration, and inability to function at their normal level of ability, but they are not clinically depressed. A normal grief reaction is not clinical depression and should not be treated as such. However, a bereaved person can also be clinically depressed. Worden states that the bereaved who were also depressed had little support, were not good problem solvers, were passive, and had a sense that they were not in control. Lazare (1979) specifies a number of indications that suggest unresolved grief. If several of these are noted, there is a strong possibility that the individual is caught in complicated grief and needs professional help:

• Depression that starts at the time of the death of the loved one, includes anxiety, guilt, fear, and a preoccupation with loss, and recurs at intervals even after the passage of many years.

• A history of unresolved grief that is evidenced with each new loss; the person is unable to talk about the deceased because the death is fresh in his or her mind even though it happened years before.

• Social impairment, in that the bereaved withdraws from relationships and activities.

• Physical complaints of discomfort in the sternum, breathing problems, or symptoms similar to the health problems of the deceased.

• Keeping the house as though the deceased were continuing to live there; aimless searching for the loved one.

Worden (1987) presented five potential causes of complicated grief reactions.

1   The nature of the attachment to the deceased. If the survivor was overly dependent, if there was an unusually close interdependent relationship, or if there were ambivalent feelings about the deceased, complications may arise. The bereaved's source of self-esteem may have been the deceased, and the survivor may feel unable to function independently. Fenichel (1945) believed that ambivalent feelings about the deceased lead to guilt. The greater the love-hate relationship, the greater the self-reproach and the greater the guilt.

2   The manner of death. Sudden death, multiple losses, or ambiguous losses, such as missing persons, may cause so much confusion and distress that the mourner may not be able to manage a normal grief reaction.

3   The personality of the bereaved. People who see themselves as weak and unable to cope or strong and above pain may not be able to allow themselves the opportunity to experience the healing feelings of a normal grief reaction.

4   The personal history of the bereaved. If there is a history of clinical depression or morbid grief reactions, there may well be a reoccurrence.

5   Social variables. Deaths that are socially stigmatized may complicate the mourning process. Suicides, homicides, deaths in prison, AIDS deaths, or drug overdoses may curtail honest discussion and active support and result in a dysfunctional adjustment to the loss.

Worden describes four forms that complicated grief can take:

1   Chronic grief. Years after the death, the bereaved have the same feelings and reactions that they had at the time of the death.

2   Delayed grief. When the grief work is not done at the time of the death, fresh sadness occurs much later, often at the time of another death or when triggered by a similar event.

3   Exaggerated grief. The grief is so intense that the bereaved is dysfunctional.

4 Masked grief. The grief is manifested through physical or mental health problems.

Parkes and Weiss (1983) identified an unexpected loss syndrome. The symptoms of unresolved grief described by Lazare and listed in this section are part of this syndrome. Worden (1991) amplifies by explaining that the bereaved may overreact to minor events, imitate the deceased, have self-destructive impulses, radically change life-styles, exclude friends, relatives, and activities that were associated with the deceased, or develop phobias about illness or death.

Wolfelt (1987) described avoidance patterns that result in unreconciled grief, caused, he thinks, by the survivors not allowing themselves to have feelings and express them, or by a support system that does not encourage the expression of feelings. He labels the avoiders as postponers, displacers, replacers, minimizers, and somaticizers. As the names imply, the postponer waits for a more convenient time to grieve; the displacer gets upset about other events and people; the replacer finds a substitute for the deceased; the minimizer insists that it was really nothing and that they are doing well; and the somaticizer translates feelings into physical pain.

McGoldrick (1991) has pointed out that some families do not mourn and move on but get caught in dysfunctional adaptations to loss. They are stuck at the time of their loss. They look to the past rather than anticipate the future. Emotionally, they do not move forward. Family relationships are frozen in time. Attempts are made to keep everything as it was at the time of the family member's death. Such families deny their pain and use escape as a defense mechanism, involving themselves in addictions, fantasy, or myth. They may select a family member to take the place of the deceased.

It can be deduced from the foregoing discussion that complicated grief in families means that the children experience problems with their grief. Worden (1993) believes that children of depressed parents have more problems resolving their grief. The vulnerable parent who has multiple stressors and problems coping with children, who lacks support, does not take charge but lets things happen, and who has fewer options because of limited education and financial resources produces the vulnerable child. If the parenting is dysfunctional, the child will flounder.

SUPPORT GROUPS

Alcoholics Anonymous (AA) was founded in 1935. This popular and successful self-help group has remained viable and is responsible for several spin-offs. Its twelve-step formula has been adapted by overeaters, drug users, the sexually abused, gamblers, and others with compulsive, self-destructive addictions. AA led the way for self-help, support, and therapy groups, which flourish across the country. Unlike AA groups, therapy groups are led by professionals trained in individual and group theory. Support groups frequently combine the skills of professionals and the knowledge of lay people who have experience with the problem being addressed. Self-help groups are also support groups but are more likely to be run by the participants. Both support groups and self-help groups are helpful and are endorsed by professionals and participants. Both are used by the bereaved.

Silverman, MacKenzie, Pettigas, and Wilson (1974) first introduced the concept of widows helping one another during a Harvard Medical School study conducted over the years 1967–1972. The study showed that widows were helped by having someone to talk with who was also widowed, who had survived the experience, who had no ulterior motives, who could openly listen and discuss problems, and who was involved with the widow on a local level. The efficacy of this self-help approach was established in further studies by Barrett (1978), Vachon (1980), and Videka-Sherman (1982).

Berezin (1982), writing about the loss of a pregnancy, recommended self-help groups to assist families as they vault the chasm from their world of grief to the world they knew before their loss. Berezin observed, however, that self-help and support groups are not universally embraced by the bereaved. Their reluctance is expressed with assertions that hearing about the tragedies of others will make them more depressed; that they do not like, nor do they fit in with, groups; and that they do not appreciate the suggestion that they need help.

Seiden and Timmons (1984) have discussed the myth that grieving should be done in private. They consider this damaging. They see the support group as helping people break out of such misguided thinking.

Osterweis, Soloman, and Green (1984) have made several points that confirm the effectiveness of support groups for the bereaved. They observed that group members identify with each other and are helped in the reciprocal relationships that characterize bereavement support groups. Because of the similarities of their experiences, the group members have specialized, first-hand knowledge of problems and can share coping techniques. The members' personal self-worth is enhanced as they recognize that all are facing like situations. Because of their common cause, the group members may become advocates for social change.

Segal, Fletcher, and Meekison (1986) conducted a survey of bereaved parents and found that they preferred the support of another parent or couple whose child had died. Toder (1986) contends that the group for grieving offers the advantage of shared experience and that while in the group, participants have the opportunity to address the impact of feelings, thoughts, and behaviors.

Stephens (1972) believes that the ability to share grief with others who have experienced loss helps to make grief tolerable. The bereavement support group fosters this possibility. Dorsel and Dorsel (1986) quote a bereaved group participant as saying, "We had fun too. It's not just tears. There is also laughter and joy. It's almost like finding a lot of best friends. Some people do understand . . . No one changes the subject. People care" (pp. 17–20).

Klass (1982) is a proponent of support groups and states that "all of the professional's activities are subordinate to the group's own process. The best indication that the professional is working effectively is that . . . attention remains focused on the processes within the group" (pp. 307–323).

Stroebe and Stroebe (1987), advocates of mutual support groups, see them as providing emotional support, validation support (in that group members learn that they are not going crazy), and instrumental support, such as instruction in household and personal tasks.

Tedeschi and Hamilton (1991) acknowledge that bereaved men are underrepresented in bereavement support groups. Their contention is that men who go to groups do so to help another person, usually their wives; that they feel they do not need help because they can cope; that they fear becoming emotionally distressed, as that would challenge their roles as provider and source of strength; and that they are uncomfortable with self-disclosure. Because of these factors, Tedeschi and Hamilton recommend that bereavement support groups be set up to attract men after the initial grieving period is over, that there be a strong male presence in the group, and that the group be designed to meet the needs of the bereaved men rather than trying to convince them that they have needs that must be met. This means that support groups should address concrete concerns by giving how-to information and instruction on self-care and coping.

Fitzgerald (1993), a children's group facilitator, recommends an educational/support group model for children because they need to learn about their grief as well as be shown how to cope with it. Following this approach, the children in this type of group learned that they were not the only ones dealing with the death of a loved one, that they could safely talk about death in the group, that feelings are real and accepted, and that there are acceptable and effective coping techniques. They grew to understand that others hurt, too, and that they can help others.

Decades of study have revealed that loss and grief affect people of all ages, both in similar and in unique ways. Many of the bereaved manage their grief constructively without outside help, but that is not necessary. Because assistance from specifically trained professionals is both available and effective, as is support from the bereaved who have survived their grief and from the newly bereaved with problems similar to theirs, the grieving no longer have to go it alone. Through education, understanding, and support bereaved people will find that they can adjust to lives without their loved ones and adjust in ways that embrace growth, change, and self-discovery.

Chapter 2

The Why and Wherefore of Bereavement Support Groups

One reason bereavement support groups abound is that there are a lot of bereaved. But the main reason for their popularity is that they work (DiGiulio, 1989).

WHAT IS A BEREAVEMENT SUPPORT GROUP?

Bereavement support comes in many packages. Bereavement support groups range from educational seminars to insight-oriented therapy groups. The element in each that makes them bereavement support groups is that they are attended by people who have experienced the loss of a significant other. The commonly held definition of a bereavement support group is that it is a group of people who get together on a regular basis and, with the help of a leader, discuss their problems adjusting to a world in which their loved ones no longer live. Because that is what we think of when we think of bereavement support groups, that is a model that we will discuss in detail in this book. We will also look at other types of effective bereavement support groups. Bereavement support can be an activity, a class, a spectator event, an entertainment, or a special occasion. People in grief give each other support while they are learning, enjoying themselves, developing new skills, and giving help to others. They talk, compare feelings about their new or unwanted challenges, and learn that their fears and reactions are a normal part of the grief process (Crenshaw, 1990). They are validated and relieved, which helps them manage the stress of adapting to new life-styles. They are meeting people, making friends, developing new hope, enhancing their self-esteem and self-confidence, and giving and receiving support.

Because a support group is typically seen as a forum for the discussion and understanding of a certain set of problems that its members are facing, having fun and making contributions to others do not seem serious enough to be of benefit. Be assured that they are. Sitting down and talking, sharing, and commiserating together make up an important method of support. The acceptance and the expression of feelings are often crucial to the healing process that allows the bereaved to move forward into a new and vital life. However, this type of grief support does not appeal to everyone, as not all of the bereaved are geared to emotional expression. Some people hate talking in a group (Haan, 1991), cannot bear to reveal their inner feelings, value privacy, and want to choose their confidants. They may be able to participate in group activities, but they cannot tolerate losing control in front of a group of people they do not know very well.

Those who work in the field of grief resolution tend to look at the openly expressive grievers as the ones who are doing it right (Schiff, 1986). There is a tendency to think that the bereaved who do not acknowledge and express their despair are grieving improperly and will suffer from this self-imposed stoicism. One of the reasons for this thinking is that the bereaved who vent their grief talk to the helpers. Since they share their feelings, their misery and their progress are apparent. It is seen that they have successfully accepted the death of their loved ones, worked through their losses, developed new identities, and enriched their lives through their suffering and survival. It is an inspiring pattern. The professional assistants to those in grief develop a strong bias that this is the right way to grieve. Thus people are encouraged to work through their grief by feeling it and fighting with it.

Yet just as one medicine does not work for everyone, so this one way of grief management does not work for everybody who has suffered loss. People and their grief are unique (Nichols & Nichols, 1975). The majority of people get through their grief in their own way and by themselves. Because there can be no rules on the length, breadth, or depth of grief, there can be no one standard against which we judge all grieving. There are many people, many losses, and many styles of grief. If everyone must fit one model, the number of people who can be helped is limited. If many models and varied approaches are used, more bereaved people can be reached. The individual will also need and want different kinds of bereavement support at different times.

If we believe in the incomparability of every individual; we believe that there is more than one way to do almost everything. The concept of right and wrong is an easy one to grasp. The concept that there is no one right way, that there is only each person's way, is more complicated, but more accurate. Each grief process is similar and different.

People in grief who appreciate the sit-down-and-talk-about-it bereavement support group will not find this support their permanent fix. After a course of mutual sharing, some may move on without further support. Others may continue to want support but in another form, such as a social group, a learning group, or a group for special interests.

Some of the bereaved are so enervated that they do not want help, cannot imagine that anything can help them, will not seek assistance, and will not respond to proffered help. They will ignore announcements of upcoming bereavement groups, discard personalized invitations requesting their attendance and demur when approached individually. Others will be able to recall how they handled loss in the past and try to use the same coping mechanisms to help themselves through their grief. If talking to others helped before, or if keeping busy or getting involved worked for them, they will use these proven techniques (Hughes, 1988). If they find that their old ways are not working, they will be open to suggestions. However, if they are not geared to talking, the talking approach will not appeal to them. Although they will reject that approach to grief resolution, they may be attracted to an activity, an opportunity to meet people, or a chance to do good.

Bereavement support groups can be anything that is helpful and supportive at any time during the period of bereavement. Needs change as mourning continues. Bereavement support can too.

Bereavement support groups should be designed to address the problems and concerns of the bereaved. That is the ideal delivery system. All kinds of bereavement support groups are helpful, but not all kinds of bereavement support group leaders are available. The leaders and organizers of the support groups will have to do what they do best. If they cannot be facilitators for talking and sharing bereavement support groups, they will have to offer the type of support they can. Some can teach, some can organize social events, some can serve as role models. Those willing to work can work at what they enjoy. If the leaders feel frustrated or inadequate, they will not be able to perform well and will not want to continue in the work.

Bereavement support groups need leaders. Leaders come in two varieties, professionals and laypeople. The professionals obtained their training in school; the lay leaders learned through personal experience. There are all sorts of combinations, such as the volunteer who is professionally trained and has experienced a loss of a significant person; the professional who has not had a personal loss but has had a great deal of experience working with death and loss; or the person, trained or untrained, who wants to help and is willing to learn (Folken, 1990a). The bottom line in any bereavement support group is that it is a support group.

The leaders make the meeting or the event possible, but they do not make the support and the healing happen. The facilitators may direct the discussion or arrange the event, but they are only facilitators. A bereavement support group can be called a therapy, self-help, educational, or talk group, but it will still be a support group because it is the bereaved, dealing with the problems of being suddenly alone, who are doing the healing of themselves and others. They want to know what others are going through, how they can help themselves get through it, and that there is hope and survival. They can learn these things from the other participants because each one will be at a different stage in the bereavement process and because everyone is different. What troubles one, another will manage well. Coping skills and sensitivities differ. The facilitator's job is to get the bereaved together and keep the group moving.

Specialized support groups for specific losses are not available in every community. It is not always possible to offer separate groups for the significant others of murder victims; for spouses, for relatives of people who commit suicide; for parents of children who die from sudden infant death syndrome (SIDS); for families of children who succumb to cancer or children who grieve for their parents or siblings; for friends and relatives of people who were killed by drunken drivers or who died of Acquired Immune Deficiency Syndrome (AIDS); for grandparents or for parents who experience a miscarriage or a stillbirth. These are all important support groups, but some communities do not have the population to maintain segregated support groups or cannot find appropriate and willing leaders.

Are specialized groups better? Does it help those in mourning to be in a group only for children or men or women, or to meet with others who have suffered losses similar to theirs? The answer is yes (Lindeman, 1983). Although no one can ever know how another person feels, those who have gone through it can know better. They share comparable experiences and have an understanding of one another's wounds. The more narrowly defined the loss, the more the group members feel the group support and think their particular losses are understood and addressed. In bereavement support groups, having grief in common is a plus that helps (Yalom, 1985). Whenever possible, specialized support groups should be offered.

Hundreds of communities have mixed bereavement groups, made up of people who have experienced different kinds of losses. Although some groups also include individuals who are struggling with the aftermath of divorce, this is not recommended and usually does not work out for either the divorced or the bereaved. Most mixed groups accept any adult who has suffered the death of a loved one, be it a parent, sibling, spouse, or other close relative or friend. Although mixed groups may not be ideal, they do offer support, and at times it is useful for the bereaved to be made aware of the many faces of grief. On occasion someone will decide that if one of the group members can manage circumstances that are overwhelming, they should have no problem with their own loss, which in comparison seems less traumatic. In areas where the population is small and facilitators have limited time, mixed groups fill a need. Most often such groups are ongoing, with members coming and going at their own discretion. Consequently, in any group there are people in various stages of bereavement. Some are in shock; others are angry; others are at the point where they are more interested in the socializing aspects of the group than in the sharing of mutual grief. That can be a problem if the cameraderie is to boisterous, but it can be a revelation for the recently bereaved to see the progress of those who are emerging from their grief.

If grief is compared—"Mine is worse than yours"—mixed groups can present a problem. But the problem can be remedied with the statement that each person's grief is the worst because everybody has to go through his or her own grief. The only thing that can be said about everybody's grief is that the grief of each one is different.

If the majority of the group wants to socialize and plan activities to enjoy, but the newcomers need to talk about their distress, the mixed group is a problem. When such a situation occurs, the newly bereaved will be turned off and will turn away. The difficulty can be addressed by encouraging those who need social support to spin off into a transitional group with different priorities. Those who want to stay to help the new participants can be invited to do so. As they help others they will find that they are also helping themselves. They will find and work at their own pockets of grief.

Some points to keep in mind:

1   All of the bereaved do not respond to the same type of grief support.
2   The bereaved need different kinds of support when they are in different stages of grief.
3   The more the bereaved have in common, the more they feel the value of the support group.

WHY HAVE BEREAVEMENT SUPPORT GROUPS

Bereavement support groups deliver help that alleviates pain but is not intrusive. Participants can use the group however they wish. It does not consume the person's life, and no prescription is required. Those who feel that the problems they are experiencing do not require psychotherapy will not have the same reluctance to attend a support group. The groups are often offered at no cost to those who attend, and no commitment is exacted. The bereaved get to talk with others who are sharing their experiences. Although they may feel that they are unable to talk with strangers, they soon determine that the people in the bereavement support group are not strangers because of the grief that they have in common. Group participants learn that they have not lost their minds and that given time and effort they will feel better (Gaver, 1976).

Emotional and Physical Relief

Bereavement support groups may save lives. They provide emotional relief and in doing so can help alleviate physical problems. They enhance the quality of life and help people find new meaning in their lives.

Finding Mentors

Men, women, and children find mentors in bereavement support groups. It may be another participant, the facilitator, or the entire group that guides and inspires the individual. The group members receive help in coping with their grief and furthering their own healing. Their lives grow as they venture in directions they never thought possible. They may pursue long-lost ambitions. Life will have renewed purpose.

Not Isolated in Grief

People going to bereavement support groups do not have to grieve alone. There is no special merit in mourning in isolation. Grief does not need to be suffered in silence and solitude.

Educational

Bereavement support groups are educational. Participants learn that grief is a process, that the sun will shine again, that certain symptoms are common, that they are not insane, that hardly anyone knows how to say and do the right thing, and that there are techniques they can use to help themselves (Osmont & Mcfarlane, 1988).

A Safe Place

Bereavement support groups give their participants a safe place to experience the pain of loss, accept the loss, adjust to the loss, and reinvest their energy into other relationships and activities. Participants learn that a down day is not a relapse and a good day is not a cure. They learn patience with themselves and with others. They can hold themselves together from meeting to meeting knowing that they have a place to go where they can talk, cry, and share (Williams, 1988). As they verbalize they hear and understand themselves and thus can better help themselves.

Information Exchange

Through the exchange of information in bereavement support groups, bereaved spouses learn that people are treating them differently not because there is anything wrong with them, but because they are now single. This information is validated by others in the support group. They learn about the facts of widowed life and know that what they perceive is reality and not paranoia.

More Resources

Bereavement support groups make it possible to spread around the caring and concern. The grieving do not become dependent on one person for everything. They can like and appreciate different people for different things. Someone may have knowledge about finances, another will have suggestions regarding safety and security, and someone else will know where to go to meet people.

Developing Interpersonal Skills

Because bereavement support group members learn to help others by being nonjudgmental, by listening, and by relating personal experiences instead of giving advice, they develop interpersonal skills. They find out that they can help others through acceptance and encouragement and end by feeling confident in themselves.

Being Accepted

Bereavement support group participants do not have to worry about the group members' reactions, about whether they are talking too much, or whether they are saying something embarrassing or hurtful. Everyone in the group understands and will welcome the sharing of feelings. They will not urge people who are sharing, crying, angry, or insecure to get a hold of themselves, get on with their lives, put it in the past, or forget it. And while individuals deal with feelings they also deal with the facts of the here and now. They work with the reality of their present travail. The support group members help each other review past values and relate them to the present. They re-evaluate and develop a system to meet the demands of their new lives. The individuals in a support group do not take on one another's problems. Although they face similar circumstances, they know that all must solve their own problems in their own way. Helping each other in this way diminishes their own feelings of helplessness and inadequacy.

Relieving Loneliness

Attending a bereavement support group and meeting others will help the
bereaved overcome some of their loneliness. Group members will never
replace the person they miss or take away their longing for the one who
died, but there will be other people to talk with while they are groping with
their aloneness (Tatelbaum, 1989).

Self-Help

Bereavement support groups take healing out of the hands of the professional and put it in the laps of those who have the expertise, the people who
have experienced the traumatic loss of loved ones (McKendree, 1989). The
bereaved know that they know what it is like to experience and grieve over a
loss and that they can provide strength for one another. Prescriptions from
professionals often frustrate rather than help because the bereaved cannot
always manage to do what they are told to do. They can, however, share
their concerns with others with similar problems and have their thoughts
and behaviors normalized by them.

Attacking Problems, Not People

In bereavement support groups the members are not seen as problems.
They may have problems, and their behaviors may be alarming, but they are
not labeled. Bereavement support groups help people come to grips with
disturbing feelings and behaviors because others in the group have had
the same experiences and understand. When they achieve a wanted
adjustment, or accomplish something new or difficult, they know that they
have done it themselves and can feel good about their abilities. Receiving
help through the support group is not the same as getting outside,
professional help. Doing well because of group support gives the bereaved
a feeling of "I did it!" When the same progress is noted after professional
help, there is the thought that they could not have done it without the
therapist. When the bereaved feel that they achieved on their own, the gains
are more likely to last.

Not All Sorrow and Tears

Bereavement support groups give the grieving a place to laugh and have
fun. They can safely laugh at themselves and see that life is not all sorrow
and tears.

Accepting Responsibilities

Through the support of the bereavement group, the participants come to
terms with what they have to do. They are angry that their children have to

go to day care while they return to work; that they have to do their own laundry and take care of the car; that they are faced with responsibilities they never had before and never wanted. The other group members share the frustration, hear the complaints, and help one another figure out how they can best do what has to be done.

Telling Their Stories

Bereavement support groups allow the necessary retelling of stories of the sickness, death, and funeral that friends, relatives, and neighbors no longer want to hear. When everyone involved in the mourning persons' lives want them to forget about it, the support group will allow them to grieve and talk about their grief for as long as they want (Caine, 1974).

Discussing Decisions

The members of bereavement support groups help each other make decisions. When a spouse dies, the survivor may have no one with whom to discuss ideas and formulate thoughts. Group members help by listening, making suggestions, and sharing knowledge.

Putting Off Decisions

Sometimes bereavement group members gain the advantage of time. They learn from others that grief takes time and that important decisions which can be put off should be (Brothers, 1990). They will be encouraged to let their attitudes settle and change and to exercise caution during this time of reorganization.

Working on Identity

The bereaved who attend support groups can develop their identity. They are not just parents, children, spouses, neighbors, or friends. Their new acquaintances will help the bereaved see themselves in new and positive ways. They discover that when their spouses died they did not lose themselves. They learn from their compatriots that they are whole people who can develop a new vision of themselves.

Discussing Frustrations

Support groups give those attending a safe place to say things that they cannot say elsewhere. They can express their frustrations with family members, their former best friends, and other acquaintances who do not seem to know how to talk with them and who manage to say and do things that make matters worse instead of better.

Bonding

People in bereavement groups come together as strangers, bond on an emotional level, and develop significant relationships. The bereavement support group provides a place where people learn that there will be other trusting and meaningful relationships in their lives.

Making New Friends

The bereavement group members find an additional group of friends. They have the people they knew before the death of their loved one, and they have the group members who are with them after the traumatic loss. Total dependency on their long-suffering support system is not good for the mourners and is not always appreciated by friends and family. Dependency on group members is accepted and encouraged. They attend the group because of the need to find help from those who know and understand. Those who attend become dependent on one another but not in a way that says, Take over and be responsible for my life. It is a healthy dependency that concentrates on the part of life that is hurting and reaching out for the person who is no longer present. Group members depend on each other as they help themselves through grief. Although they depend on the group members for solace, they select particular members for individual contact. Those special friends are chosen because they have something extra to offer: they can be trusted with confidential information, they can be companions in mutual pursuits, or they are people who cheer one up or are easy to talk with. This dependency is sound because it is not all-encompassing; it is a mutual dependency and a vehicle for growth.

Pride in Progress

Bereavement support groups help members to feel that they are doing something to help themselves. They know that they are attacking the problem by learning about it, experiencing it, taking some action, and moving away from the status quo. It is an unsure but proud time. When they help themselves, other possibilities arise.

Support That Helps

Studies have shown that those who have the support of other widowed persons are better able to adjust to widowhood (Parkes, 1980). Bereavement groups bring the widowed together to help one another, to share concerns, and to feel support. They know that the others in the group have no ulterior motives, are not giving pat answers, are not trying to plan their lives for them, and are not giving them professional opinions (Farra, 1986).

Sharing What Works

In bereavement groups those who attend can learn about other resources available to them, such as transportation services, entertainment, and who does good work on the house, the yard, or the car. Since the group members have usually tried what they recommend, the widowed have more confidence in the recommendations.

Learning to Cope

The bereavement group members teach each other how to cope. Not only is there an exchange of helpful resources and information, there are words of wisdom. They encourage one another to try new things or to protect themselves from people who make them uncomfortable. They help each other with techniques for getting through the day by taking one day at a time, deciding what does not need immediate attention, and suggesting approaches for asking people to help them.

Substituting For Loss

Although bereavement groups cannot replace all that is lost when a spouse dies, they can provide companionship, a confidant, acceptance, a social circle, a safe harbor, and a place for the bereaved to find their identities as single people.

Long-Term Availability

Ongoing bereavement groups are valuable in that they give support for the long run. Friends and family members may become weary of giving support, but ongoing bereavement groups are there to be used for as long as is necessary.

Happy Memories

Bereavement support groups are good places for those who have experienced a traumatic loss to live through the pain of the bad memories and get back to the pride and poignancy of the good memories.

Work on Hidden Problems

In a bereavement support group the participants can find out what is bothering them. They may feel pain and distress but be unable to verbalize their unhappiness because they do not understand it. As the facilitator and the group members talk about feelings, these participants will develop insight into their problems. The group leader or other group members will also bring up problems that some of the attendees may have been reluctant to talk about or embarrassed to mention. When an issue is out in the open, people feel freer to discuss it; they are comforted to know that others have cares similar to theirs.

No "Shoulds"

Being heard nonjudgmentally is a luxury in our culture. Although suggestions may be given, there are no "shoulds" in bereavement groups. Being heard and accepted, no matter what, is a wonderful gift.

GROUP SUPPORT IDEAS

The following are examples of nontraditional bereavement support. The groups that I will describe have been used successfully with the widowed population but can be adapted to other groups of bereaved, as will be discussed following the description of the activity.

A Walk on the Beach

A "walk on the beach" can be adapted to any area of the country. It might be a walk in the mall, a stroll in the park, a climb up a hill, a meander through the forest, or a ride down the river or around the lake.

A hospice nurse, who was herself widowed, volunteered to start a regular walk on the beach. The walk was sponsored by the Hospice of the Treasure Coast and was open to any widowed person who wanted to attend. No reservations were required. All the widowed were invited through the community calendar published weekly in the local newspaper, and the activity was also publicized in the hospice newsletter. Participants were asked to meet in the late afternoon at a certain place in the local state park; they were encouraged to bring a sandwich and a drink so that they could picnic together before the walk down the beach. People could go if they felt like it, eat and run, arrive just in time for the walk, or sit and look at the view until the walkers returned. They could reach out and develop relationships, or they could withdraw from personal revelations (Campbell and Silvermam, 1987). The group was made up of men and women who had been widowed years ago or only weeks ago. Some of them were initially accompanied by their children, friends, or other relatives. But once they became part of the group and developed new relationships, they no longer needed their escorts.

Some of the widowed used this outing as an adjunct to other support from ongoing or closed-end support groups. Some had supportive friends and relatives in the community but felt a need to make contacts among the widowed, feeling a need to meet single people.

For some of the widowed, the picnic and trip to the beach enlarged their lives. They had not been on such a jaunt for ages and loved the atmosphere and setting. Many were proud that they could go someplace on their own. Because they all were welcomed, their efforts at reaching out were given positive reinforcement. Other participants used the occasion to make friends who could accompany them to other events. Several of the widows and widowers dated, got to like each other very much, and paired off. They all received support, even though it was not a structured support group.

This type of support group is good for all ages, for men, women, and in general for people who appreciate action over talking. It can readily adapt to the needs of the younger widowed accompanied by their children. People can enlarge their circle of friends, receive support, and have a pleasant and safe outing.

An Educational Seminar

A one- or two-hour educational seminar presented to a group of bereaved people is a remarkable form of bereavement support because a presentation on the normal grief reaction is amazingly consoling. It offers the same consolation that anyone would feel if they thought they had a terminal disease, that there was nothing that could be done for them, and no reason to have hope, and they then learned that their sickness was not life-threatening, that treatments were available that would give relief, and that they had every reason to hope that they would improve.

The seminar is programmed to let the bereaved know that what they are undergoing is normal—that they are not stuck in a permanent depression, are not losing their minds, and that in time they will regain their mental acuity and physical strength. As they see other bereaved people nod in understanding, and hear the discussion, they gain energy and relief. This information, liberally laced with true anecdotes about others who have grieved successfully, gives them reason to feel hopeful about their own survival. A few pointers about what they can do to help themselves will aid the bereaved in their progress away from helplessness and toward hopefulness. If the seminar is long enough to include a break, it will augment the support, as the "students" will be able to talk about what they have learned without having to reveal themselves. It is much easier to chat about the teacher's lesson than it is to let out one's fears and worries. If the seminar is not long enough to justify a break, offering refreshments at the end of the lecture permits those attending to talk to one another. Ongoing seminars work well as the basis of a bereavement support group because sharing in a "classroom" is much less threatening than sharing in a support group set up for that purpose. If different topics are presented at each seminar, the same group will continue to attend. The attendees will get to know each other and will gain an interdependence that will start with looking forward to seeing one another at the next seminar, lead to the sharing of rides, and continue into new friendships.

This type of bereavement support group is good for adult men and women. It works for the widowed of all ages, for grieving parents, siblings and other relatives, and friends. It can have a very positive impact on bereaved teenagers if they can be persuaded to attend. It is particularly helpful for people who want to solve problems intellectually rather than emotionally. For them, learning about their problem is less distressing than talking about the problem. As they learn, they will understand that their painful feelings are normal and will eventually subside (Staudacher, 1987). People who do not want to talk about their problems can talk about "symptoms" when the symptoms are given a name, attached to a process, and taught by a legitimate instructor.

In a seminar series, one finds that the same bereaved people keep coming and that they end up talking to each other rather than listening to the teacher. Consequently, if there is material that is thought to be essential it should be presented as early as possible. Toward the end, the instructor becomes a facilitator, as the bereaved talk to each other about themselves.

A Potluck Dinner

Potluck dinners need to be sponsored by a church group, a senior center, or a volunteer organization, or be arranged at the end of a closed-end bereavement group or as a special session of an open-ended group. There has to be a reason and an available group before people will attend. A meeting of strangers bringing food to share is not alluring to the bereaved or to anyone else (Loewinsohn, 1979).

Potlucks are supportive because eating is a social occasion in this culture and generates a feeling of camaraderie. It gives an excuse for overindulging and is an opportunity for some "home-cooking." Potlucks are good endings for traditional, talking bereavement support groups because they help the participants move on to socializing and nurturing themselves and others.

Potlucks are appropriate for male and female adults, for the outgoing as well as those who tend to turn inward. Eating is a natural occurrence that is enjoyable both to those who prepare the food and to those who benefit from its availability. While eating, people are not under pressure to talk, but there is a supply of ready-made subjects, such as compliments to the cook. An occasion with food gives those who are struggling with shopping, meal preparation, and eating an opportunity to discuss their problems without the pressure of a group of participants focusing on them while they make their needs known.

All ages—men and women, parents, friends, and children—can appreciate potluck get-togethers. They are effective for mixed groups; grieving families can attend and meet others facing similar challenges. There is security and comfort in the numbers and in the ordinariness of the activity.

A Group Outing

The bereaved who have not been accustomed to going out by themselves feel socially deprived. If they attempt to dine out alone or attend an event without a companion, they feel overwhelmingly bereft, as their losses are brought home to them. They wonder if they will have to forgo previously pleasurable entertainments or if they will never be able to develop interests they thought they might enjoy. In this couple-oriented society, the widowed are not routinely invited to accompany married friends. A group outing gives the widowed the opportunity to try something new or to continue activities that they formerly pursued with a spouse. It spurs them to get going because the event is arranged for them. They learn that being a couple is not the only way to go. They may become interested in something they never cared for before, and they will make friends in a nonthreatening setting. They can be as gregarious or as withdrawn as they want to be, can bring up their problems as they talk to others, or listen and learn as they overhear what their coparticipants are saying.

Group outings to plays, dinners, lunches, sports events, festivals, musical programs, or other community events get the widowed back into the mainstream of activity. They practice their social skills while enjoying themselves. They will do things they never thought possible, and their lives will take on new meaning.

A bereavement coordinator for a hospice arranged cruises and trips to Las Vegas for bereaved spouses who were being helped through his organization (Monahan, 1993). The participants had a wonderful time. They were thrilled at being able to handle themselves in new situations, made friends, and discussed the many challenges of widowhood while dining, drinking, traveling, and playing.

Another group of widowed people organized themselves as a weekly luncheon group after their closed-end bereavement group ended. If a member failed to show up, one of the group called to let them know they were missed; it was good for them to know that others cared. As the group became more involved with one another, they planned monthly outings to plays, sports events, and musical programs. One person took responsibility for setting the date and time and making the reservations. They rotated this responsibility monthly so each one had the experience of being the manager. Since reservations were required, the widowed were obligated to plan ahead. It gave them something to look forward to and was a pleasant way for them to obtain support while being forced to make decisions.

A group of this kind will also work for the bereaved who are not widowed, but are parents, friends, and relatives. Survivors of all kinds of losses will enjoy a luncheon meeting if they are employed or a weekend trip if children are involved. It is supportive to be reminded that life can be fun and that interesting pursuits are available.

A Breakfast Get-Together

A breakfast get-together is good for the bereaved who are retired and also provides group support for bereaved people working in jobs. A regularly scheduled breakfast group has been a mainstay of the bereavement support programs of the Widowed Persons Services in Rochester, Minnesota (Monson, 1985), and Denver, Colorado. The men's group in Rochester meets weekly because the members found that one time a month was too confusing for men who had lost their "social secretaries."

The group in Denver, which has been in operation since 1987, meets weekly at 7:30 AM in a restaurant where a room is reserved for the group. Two widowed men volunteered to be responsible for the arrangements, publicity, and record keeping. Often both men attend, but if one cannot be there, the other is. It is a place for men to meet to talk about their problems and losses and handle grief any way they want. The participants do not have to fit any grief mold; they can express themselves in their own way or not at all. The leaders found that the men who came brought other men. The two who lead this breakfast group say that widowed men have different needs than widowed women. The breakfast routine works well for them because they can come as they please, there is no obligation, they do not have to reciprocate, and they know the group is always there. The men who attend know that the other widowers understand what they are facing as they struggle to adjust to life without a mate. The leaders also learned that they had to be tuned in to the newly widowed, who were not at the same stage emotionally as those who had been attending longer. Newcomers are given the opportunity for individual sharing with one of the group members. In a similar breakfast group in Iowa, new participants are given a heart sticker so that everyone in the group can identify them and give them special attention.

A place to go where widowers are always welcome and where they can be around other widowers is supportive. There is no expectation that the bereaved act in any one way. They know that they can talk about the weather, the ball game, the crabgrass, or their dead wives. They are allowed and encouraged to use the breakfast group in their own ways.

This type of group appears to be particularly effective with widowed men, young and old. Nevertheless, it is conceivable that other groups of survivors would also find the format supportive. It may be particularly appealing to busy people who have many responsibilities.

Games or Cards

The same nurse who started the walk on the beach group also started a monthly game time in her home. A group that included widowed people from her church and hospice survivors met once a month at her house to have a snack and play games. This activity was comfortable for the socially awkward, as it gave them something to do. They did not have to make small talk or worry that they would look like a dunce or be a wallflower. Because only the widowed would be there, they knew that the others would understand if they appeared forgetful or tearful. The widows used this opportunity to practice their social skills and to expand their social life.

Such a group works well for the widowed who want to be around others but cannot remember what it was like to socialize on their own. Because everyone in the group is single, they do not feel as though they stand out. It is a good first step toward getting involved in more groups with more people. The participants do not have to talk about their bereavement, but they can if they want to. Even if they say nothing, they can listen and quietly compare their own problems with those of others.

This type of group is good for the bereaved of all ages and is particularly helpful for those who like a structured situation. Those who went to this nurse's home knew what they could expect. They saw many of the same people, played the same games, and always met at the same day and time. The socially inept did not have to worry about what to say and do. This was their opportunity to redevelop their social skills so they could move on to other companionable situations. Although this group is described as meeting the needs of adults, it is also supportive for children. Play groups for children who have experienced traumatic loss are particularly appropriate.

In a Widowed Persons Service program in a large city, a widowed outreach volunteer invited a group of widowers to his home to play poker. It developed into a regular weekly outing. They played poker, talked, and built trust. In time, the poker game became an excuse for the get-together. The time was used to play a little cards, talk a lot, and learn skills such as cooking, cleaning, shopping, and how to do the laundry. It was exactly the kind of bereavement support that these men needed, but it would not have developed had they not had poker as their entree.

Games are especially suitable for a bereavement support group because of the socializing and congeniality that take place. But it never stops at that. When people who have a similar problem get together, they inevitably talk about that problem. They support each other.

A One-Topic Quasi-Educational Group

Bereaved people are reluctant to seek help for some of their problems that they consider personal or embarrassing, or which they have not conceptualized well enough to allow asking for help. Group meetings with a guest speaker and a hot topic entice many people who are in such a situation. The Grand Rapids, Michigan, Widowed Persons Service, an all-volunteer organization, recruited speakers to address subjects that the volunteers, all widows themselves, knew were troubling the widowed. In August, September, and October 1991, the group announced talks on the following topics: Changing Old Habits; Single, Sexy, Celibate?; Growth Through Loss; Stress and Loss; Financial Matters; Family Response to Loss; Your Social Well-Being; and Use of Medications During Bereavement. The topics were generally educational but were also subjects of immediate interest to the bereaved. The talks were quasi-educational because they also included opportunities for interaction, discussion, and the relating of personal experiences, both during and at the end of the presentations.

Such series of talks are particularly effective for the impatient bereaved who do not want to listen to others talk about problems that they think have no bearing on their own. Their concerns can be addressed and they can participate with enthusiasm because the group meeting touches on what they want to talk about. Special-topic bereavement groups will bring out people who would not tolerate groups devoted to nonspecific emotional sharing. They will receive information and support that they would otherwise miss because of their low tolerance for the problems of other people. Sometimes a topic is of such pressing interest to the widowed that the presentation actually draws too many people to allow open discussion. Such a situation can be prevented by requesting that reservations be made. A larger number can be accommodated if the speaker addresses the entire group and the audience then breaks up into smaller discussion groups. In another variation, the large group can be followed with scheduled parleys on the topic at a later meeting. This is one way to bring new members to an ongoing, talk-centered bereavement support group: people may find that they like the discussion format.

Although these topics are designed for the widowed, this type of group support can be specifically organized for any group of people in grief, such as parents, AIDS survivors, relatives of suicide victims, and relatives of homicide victims.

The bereaved who will welcome this approach are those who like to solve problems by learning as much as they can about them.

A Craft or Hobby Class

Quilting parties and barn-raisings were opportunities to get together and talk long before specialized support groups came into existence. Many people are more comfortable talking if they are involved in an activity. A joint project that keeps the hands busy will free the mind and mouth for spontaneous conversation. When a class is made up of people who are bereaved, the conversation naturally turns to the problems of adjusting to life without the loved one. Additionally, the completion of a project gives a feeling of accomplishment. When lives are in trauma, being able to see a project through to the end is an organizing achievement (Stearns, 1984). Classes can be planned to appeal to both men and women or can be particular to the interests of either.

This type of bereavement support is also good for children, who are more likely to reveal their thoughts, feelings, and concerns through activity (Kübler-Ross, 1983). Music, art, and dance therapy can be used to help children symbolically vent their fears and troubles when important people in their lives die. Adults can make use of this approach as well. If prospective group members shy away from the word *therapy,* call it an interpretive music class, mood music, art class, art expression, dance theory, or free-form dance. Once they get involved the name will be insignificant. They will have a good time while encouraging each other and venting their feelings.

A Group Volunteer Effort

Doing something for others is a stress-relieving activity. It is altruistic egoism (Selye, 1976) because in helping others the bereaved find that they help themselves. Not all volunteer work is suited to all people, whether it is because of personalities and inclinations, or because of recent experience with a loved one's sicknesses and death. However, if bereaved people are able to do something for others, it is a supportive experience for them. Some excellent self-help takes place when groups of bereaved people gather to assist in a volunteer effort. They may prepare mailings, plan fund-raising events, or attend volunteer orientation programs. As they work and talk, they heal. They support each other in their mutual concern, in a casual manner, while performing worthwhile work.

Many people believe that merely talking about something will not do any good, that it takes action to fix anything. People who have this conviction need purposeful activity to occupy them. If they can be occupied and, at the same time, talk about the problems they face as bereaved people, they will start feeling better. They will think their "busy-ness" and exertions caused the improvement; they will develop an attachment to the people they talked with and demonstrate more openness in their dealings with others.

A Dance

There comes a point in many bereavements when socializing is more supportive than verbalizing, no matter how helpful and instructive the discussions might be. The activity does not have to be a dance, but it is good to arrange something that is fun, that is definitely social, and that encourages interaction with many people. A dance planned in a way that encourages single, unaccompanied people to attend is recommended. The more people who attend and dance, the merrier the occasion. It is supportive to learn that life can be joyful, that there are laughs to be had, and that it is possible for the newly single to function well in social situations.

Timing is important. Many bereaved are not ready for gaiety early on and may be repelled by contemporaries who seem too lighthearted. They see themselves caught in a serious situation and need to work on their sorrow rather than their social life. When they are able to come out of their grief enough to look around and see what they are missing, they will appreciate social opportunities.

A Day of Remembrance

Many hospices have organized yearly days of remembrance, when all the survivors of the past year's patients are invited to attend a ceremony that honors those who died. The names are read; appropriate readings and songs are presented; there may be a candle-lighting ritual. Hospice workers whom the families worked with and know take part in the observance. The participants are invited to stay for food and fellowship afterward. It is a moving and meaningful service, a sharing that transcends words. Men, women, and children find the day of remembrance a touching and healing event. They share the experience as a family, with friends and with the professional caregivers. It is an opportunity to say thank you, good-bye, and now it is up to me. It is bereavement support. Mausoleum and cemetery associations have also begun to offer yearly memorial services.

Special Skills Training

After a traumatic loss people feel more vulnerable. They may not be, but they nevertheless feel that they are. Consequently, anything they can learn that will make them feel safer is supportive. The bereaved want to know about home security features, how to avoid scams, about financial investments, how to complete minor repairs, how to manage a household, and how to travel safely. While they learn, they talk, exchange information, and share common concerns. Surviving-single classes have been turning points for many of the widowed. Self-defense skills are a boon to the bereaved of all ages. People who have lost loved ones through violence particularly need knowledge about safety measures.

A Party

The newly bereaved will not be in the mood for a party and may cringe at the idea. But withdrawal does not last forever, and a party can be just the support that bereaved people need when they are ready to emerge from their self-isolation. Any kind of party is good, but those that observe special holidays are particularly appropriate. It is hard for the bereaved to face holidays without their loved ones who have died. Learning new holiday traditions while making new friends is important and supportive. Think about theme parties for Valentine's Day; the Christmas, Hanukkah, and New Year's season; Thanksgiving; Easter; and other occasions observed in your area. Emotions will be felt, shared, and accepted; people will experience strong, poignant, and pleasant feelings. They will understand that others care and will take another step toward a new life-style.

These activities bring the bereaved together for exercising, learning, eating, socializing, volunteering, playing, remembering, celebrating, sharing, and most of all for meeting each other and getting into routines suited for their single lives.

SOME PROBLEMS WITH BEREAVEMENT SUPPORT GROUPS

With all these reasons for offering bereavement support groups to those in grief, it would seem the treatment of choice. Yet as helpful as the groups are and as much as we may want the bereaved to avail themselves to them, not all will be willing to attend a group meeting, nor will all find group support the answer to their problems. In fact, the majority of the bereaved do not seek help. They manage by themselves, relying on the support system and the coping skills that they have used all their lives.

Hospice organizations, which have access to many survivors because they have been involved with families during the illness of the deceased, report that from 10% to 15% of the bereaved need or want additional support after the death. They receive requests for tangible help, such as filing insurance forms. Some survivors will want one-to-one contact with a bereavement counselor but their immediate problems can be quickly solved.

Some of the bereaved may be unsuited for the support-group approach because of personal, emotional, physical, or environmental problems that require more help and individual attention that can be delivered in a group setting. Their distressing problems take away from, rather than augment, what the other participants get out of the group. Others cannot tolerate a group setting and find association with people in sorrow depressing and stigmatizing. They want and need to be with individuals in various life roles who can stimulate other thoughts and activities.

There are the bereaved who are harmed by attending support groups. They are people who do not relate well to others, have no clear self-image, and constantly compare themselves unfavorably to others. Reports and suggestions from group members are defeating rather than beneficial for them.

Some people are too dependent to work successfully in a support group. Their passivity and desire to have someone else take over for them will either play into the caretaking needs of other group members or repel them. Dependent participants will not achieve what they want because the group does not offer it. They will feel shunned by the participants who cannot or do not want to take on other participants' problems. The dependent person's problems will detract from the benefits that can accrue to the rest of the group because of the anger, pity, or concern the others feel for the needy group member.

When group members feel pressured to follow a grief model suggested by the facilitator or modeled by the majority of the participants, they will be uncomfortable and may conclude they are grieving incorrectly.

DISSATISFACTION AND DANGER
IN POORLY DEFINED GROUPS

Bereavement support groups go wrong when they try to be something they are not. Bereavement support groups are designed to give support during bereavement. This role does not preclude the participants from reaping other benefits and making personal gains. It does mean, however, that the facilitator and the participants should not try to achieve personality changes or treat emotional disorders. Those must be left to therapy groups set up for the purpose. The individual and group goals must be clear so there is no confusion. Any group leader who goes beyond the mission of the group is trespassing into areas not authorized by the group members. Any participants who expect more than bereavement support need to understand that the help they seek is elsewhere.

In 1977 Galinsky and Schopler did a study on casualties of the group approach based on their own observations and the reports of other professionals. Their comprehensive review of the social work and social science literature found that lack of structure and operating procedures led to problems. When clarity regarding the norms was missing, there was low task orientation. When the leader and other group members were confrontational, coercive, or attacked the defenses of the participants, distress and damage resulted. They suggested that these problems could be avoided by carefully preparing the prospective group members so that they would know what to expect. They stressed paying close attention to the composition of the group, so that there would not be extreme differences among members, as well as the importance of the leader's maintaining professional objectivity. Galinsky and Schopler undertook another study on negative group experiences in 1981, gathering information through telephone interviews. They were alarmed by participants' complaints of being pressed to reveal too much too soon. Group members expected to be protected by facilitators when group standards failed to safeguard them. It was their conviction that the leader should be knowledgeable about group dynamics and step in when corrections needed to be made. They contended that clear group and individual goals would prevent bad outcomes.

Gains Through Group Experience

The positives nevertheless outweigh the negatives, and bereavement support groups are the treatment of choice for many. Even though only a small percentage of the bereaved attend bereavement support groups, those who do become confirmed supporters of the approach, speaking of their gains in emotional understanding and control, contacts with others, and self-esteem. This word-of-mouth publicity is the best form of recruitment there is and shows that bereavement support groups need to be available in the community.

Chapter 3

Getting Them to Come

Offering a wonderful service is not enough. People need to hear about it at the time they need it and be motivated to make the effort to use the service (Bartlett & Radabaugh, 1987).

Organizations offering bereavement support groups to a built-in clientele fare better in reaching prospective participants. Hospice agencies and funeral homes draw from ready-made groups. They have the names, addresses, and telephone numbers of the people with whom they have done business. They have contact with the bereaved and can approach them because they are trusted providers. They have the service, the people, and the need all together at the right time and can offer extras that will overcome the barriers that would prevent attendance.

Other organizations reach out to the bereaved through means such as advertising and personal contact. Widowed Persons Service volunteers obtain the names of the widowed through referrals, obituaries, and agencies and contact them by mail and telephone. Although Widowed Persons Service outreach volunteers do not have the benefit of knowing potential participants before they are widowed, they have something special to offer in that all of the outreach volunteers are themselves widowed. This is their entree into the lives of people they have never met before: They have experienced and survived being widowed. Because of what they have been through, they have a good understanding of what the newly bereaved are experiencing. The bereaved they contact give them credit for knowing what they are talking about.

Personal contact continues to be the most effective means of enlisting participants for bereavement support groups. If the bereaved are not known because of services previously provided to them and the callers cannot identify themselves as knowledgeable because of personal experiences, the sponsoring organizations will have to be able to suggest some other legitimate reason for being interested and able to provide bereavement services. Health care agencies, funeral homes, and volunteer organizations such as Widowed Persons Service have justifiable motives for offering help to people in grief. Other organizations that are seen as creditable providers are churches, employee assistance programs, schools, hospitals, family service and mental health agencies, and branches of the military service. Throughout the country organizations created to help people in grief have been set up. These are called "centers for grief and loss" or "centers for loss and life transitions." The tie to bereavement services is announced in the names of these organizations. Publicity is more easily achieved and legitimacy more readily accorded if the bereavement services are tied to a known organization. If the bereaved are looking for support services, they will first contact the most logical sources.

Publicity and outreach must be constant and ongoing if the bereaved are to know of the services available to them. People pay little attention to advertising and information geared to the bereaved if they are not in that category. Publicity will capture their interest only at the time when they are bereaved and searching for help (Blackshear, 1993).

Groups that offer bereavement services will also have to overcome the newly bereaved person's fear of new experiences and lack of motivation. Many will not have the energy or the confidence to seek assistance or respond to offers of help.

The organizations and individuals that want to reach the bereaved must communicate well enough to let them know that they can provide support that is in addition to, and different from, that provided by friends, families, neighbors, and religious organizations. The suppliers of bereavement support must also make clear while they are offering comfort and guidance that the bereaved do not have to be mentally deranged to benefit from these services.

In summary, publicity must reach the people who need bereavement services when they need them, offer easy access, and demonstrate that the service offers something other than what the regular support system already provides. The description of services should sound as though it can help the bereaved free themselves from their pain while enhancing their lives.

THE NEWS MEDIA

The mass media—newspapers, radio, and television—provide wide coverage. If the bereaved do not read newspapers or listen to the radio or television, someone who cares about them will. The right message in the right place at the right time will draw people who need help to where they can get that help. Because it is hard to identify precisely the right place, time, and message, organizations that advertise want to know the sources of referrals. If a certain ad brings people in, it will be continued. If no one notices a message or advertising spot, it will be discontinued. The timing of much media publicity cannot be controlled, but effectiveness can be noted. If a feature article in the newspaper brings in 20 requests for service, and a spot on television brings in none, it is easy to determine which medium should be emphasized. No services can be provided if no one comes. People cannot come if they do not know about a program. Therefore, use every possible resource to reach those who need to know about the program. Find out what publicity reaches the targeted population and concentrate on that forum. Try other sources periodically to learn whether the market and the media have changed.

Once you have success with any of the professional newspeople, make a note of their names and numbers so that you can keep them posted on a regular basis.

Newspapers

The best publicity is free. It is called news. Do not be shy or modest about getting out the word. Use every section of the newspaper to publicize bereavement groups.

If a new person is hired to facilitate or coordinate the bereavement program, make an announcement in the business section of the newspaper. If you have information or statistics that show the value of bereavement support, or if you have participants who are willing to talk about how the support group benefited them, contact a reporter in the life-style section of the newspaper. If your organization receives funds through sponsoring a golf tournament, a marathon, a walkathon, a fishing tournament, or any sports-related event, contact the sports reporter of the newspaper. The society section will carry information about fashion shows, cocktail parties, and balls given to raise money. Volunteer awards make news. Groundbreaking ceremonies may be reported in the feature section of the newspaper. Write letters to the editor expressing appreciation and acknowledging help. Respond to a news item that relates to the bereaved, mentioning the services available from the grief support organization.

Make sure that all ongoing support groups are listed in the community activity calendar in the newspaper. Send the paper articles and pictures about the program. If what you send is interesting, the paper may print it or send a reporter to obtain more information. Always get signed releases from people mentioned in articles or pictured in photographs (Kelly, 1985).

The following are some ideas for newspaper feature stories:

1   Stories about volunteers.
2   Announcements of new support groups, who should come, and what will happen when they do.
3   Success stories about people who attended bereavement support groups.
4   Outreach efforts to contact the bereaved.
5   Anniversary celebrations or announcements about how long support groups have been offered or how many people have attended over a given period.
6   Social events sponsored by or for the bereaved.
7   Information about the topics covered in support groups.
8   The hiring of a new staff member; employee promotions, honors, awards, or accomplishments.
9   Research findings showing the effectiveness of bereavement support.
10   Fund-raising events.
11   Expansions of services
12   New volunteers or volunteer training.
13   Conferences attended by staff; knowledge gained that is of interest to the general public.

The more people involved in each event, the more newsworthy it is. If it is a topic that interests a large number of the newspaper subscribers, the editor will give it higher visibility.

If you receive a better response from the people at one local newspaper than from others, be sure to stay on good terms with them by offering them first chance at any story you have. But do not neglect other area newspapers or specialty newspapers and newsletters. Many localities have newspapers devoted to senior citizens, families, or employees of certain organizations. Churches and chambers of commerce have newsletters and bulletins. So do many agencies and companies that employ a large number of people. Anything that can be printed in the daily paper will also appeal to the smaller papers. The article or item of interest can be tailored to appeal to their readers. The editors of newsletters will be happy to get news that they can use; they usually do not have reporters and must accumulate and write all the news themselves. It is conceivable that a weekly or monthly column would be well received. Such a vehicle could include information about grief, grief recovery, and anecdotal information.

High school and college newsletters are appropriate for announcements of bereavement support groups. Statistics bring the reality of death closer to home, for example, the fact that 1 in 20 children are personally affected by the death of a loved one each year. A particularly effective time for letting schoolchildren know about grief support is when there is a highly publicized death of a young person. The announcement can include some helpful information and a telephone number that they can call for more facts and support. This information will also reach their parents and grandparents. This is also a good time to write letters to the editor. In a time of community crisis, the letter may well trigger a feature article, which in a small community may mean front-page news.

Designate someone who is free to give a rapid response to reporters. Newspaper employees work with constant deadlines. If they cannot achieve contact quickly, they will move on to other people and other stories. There may also need to be a back-up person appointed so that such opportunities are not missed. Someone needs to be available to follow up on any news story. It is good policy, too, to let the reporter and editor know how the article helped the bereavement support program and what was particularly appreciated. Include an added fact or piece of information, as it may give them ideas for future stories about the program.

Radio

A radio station is a bonanza of free publicity, particularly if it has a local interview show. The bereavement support service can come to the attention of a broad public through such a program, participation in which can be pursued regularly from different angles. Experts on bereavement can give information. People who lead the support groups can describe the process. Bereaved people who have been helped or who are attending support groups can be enlisted to talk about the personal benefits they have experienced.

Any upcoming event can be shared with radio newspeople. They will appreciate your input, and the bereavement program will profit from the publicity. Make the station personnel aware of an event two weeks prior to the date it is to occur, and keep them updated with new information, such as how many are planning to attend, clarifications, of questions asked, and new tidbits, to make the item sound fresh or more interesting. Let them know how the event went after it is over, and give them further facts about future plans. Always follow up with a thank you call and/or letter emphasizing how the station's personnel contributed to the success of the event. A letter to the reporter with a copy to the boss is a nice touch.

Public service announcements, called PSAs, are the community service element of radio programming. Broadcasters often make public appeals over the airways asking that nonprofit organizations contact them.

Table 3.1 A Public Service Announcement

TIME: 20 SECONDS   CONTACT PERSON:
                          TELEPHONE:

THE ADJUSTMENT TO LOSS CENTER SPONSORS BEREAVEMENT SUPPORT GROUPS
FOR EVERYONE IN THE COMMUNITY WHO HAS EXPERIENCED THE DEATH OF AN
IMPORTANT PERSON IN THEIR LIVES. SUPPORT GROUPS ARE HELD IN CONVENIENT
LOCATIONS SO THAT EVERYONE CAN AVAIL THEMSELVES OF THIS FREE PUBLIC
SERVICE.
CALL 1-800-008-8000 FOR MORE INFORMATION.

The radio station will accept announcements about bereavement programs and relay the message to its listeners at regular intervals. Not only will newspeople give the program free publicity, but they will read the words supplied to them. Find out the names of the station's public service directors; contact them directly and deliver your typed public service announcment to them. Give them no more than two PSAs at a time. Type them out in capital letters, one PSA to a page, triple spaced. Include the amount of time the announcement will take and the program's contact person's name and telephone number. Plan to revise the announcements every three months. The broadcast statements can range in length from 20 seconds to one minute. Twenty seconds would be about eight typed lines. A 30-second script is around nine typewritten lines. A minute-long informational is approximately 15 lines.

Each PSA should include "who, what, when, where and how." Your PSA may look like that shown in Table 3.1.

Announcements might mention that transportation can be arranged, when support groups are scheduled, the locations of groups, more specific information about symptoms of grief that can be helped by support groups, or information on other activities and services. The radio spot might also include interesting statistics, such as the number of widowed in the community (0.5% of the total population of the area), the number of children in the United States who experience the death of a parent each year (315,000), or the increased death rate of widowers compared with married men in the same age group (6 times more from heart disease; 4 times more from suicide; 3 times more from auto accidents; 10 times more from strokes).

Local radio stations often announce a community calendar. Give them specific times, dates, places, and telephone numbers, as well as a concise description of your event. Generally they do not announce regular meetings or services, but they might use a PSA for a one-time fund-raiser, the start of a new group, or a special event such as a volunteer luncheon.

Once you have made contact with a media person who is responsive, ask for advice. Then be sure to use it.

Television

What works with the newspaper and radio also works with television: Find contact people and keep those people up-to-date. Give them interesting information that they can announce or use in a news feature. Volunteer to appear on talk shows or to announce an upcoming event personally.

Television stations will also carry public service announcements, but they will have to fit the needs of the medium. A written script carrying the announcement is not effective for television because television's emphasis is on the visual. The programmers probably will accept a well-done, professional looking short video that advertises the support services the organization offers (Dickson, 1990). Some of the smaller local stations will supply a camera person, assistance with the script, and a professional announcer for the speaking part of the program. The bereavement support program will only have to provide the information and the actors. Investigate the possibility. Assistance may be available for the asking.

The program department of the American Association of Retired Persons (AARP) publishes a succinct and effective booklet called the "Public Relations Manual for Program Volunteers," which explains the who, what, when, where, why, and how of working with the news media (AARP, 1986).

SELF-GENERATED PUBLICITY

Organizations do not have to rely on the mass media to get the word out. There is much that can be done in-house. Advertising is expensive in both time and money. If an agency had no limitations on either, anything and everything could be tried. Because no organization ever seems to have more time and money than it needs, budget and personnel allocation are significant considerations. It becomes important to determine what kind of advertising is most effective. What reaches the most bereaved people? What brings results? Advertising for the sake of advertising is a waste of resources. Carefully determine what to say, who to say it to, and how to say it. Evaluate each advertising effort, and refine the advertising plan until it produces the results you want. The word thrown around in advertising circles is *targeting*. Target your market.

Brochures

Brochures must look professional enough to give prospective bereavement support group members a feeling of confidence; they should not be so obviously expensive that the recipients wonder why so much money is put into advertising instead of into services for people. The brochures should contain enough information to answer the readers' immediate questions but not so much that they bog down in all the words (Staudacher, 1987). Brochures are means to accomplish certain goals:

• To let the community know that bereavement support services are available.
• To entice the people who need bereavement support services to contact the organization that is offering them.
• To let prospective attendees know whom to call and how to get involved.

Continue to think "who, what, when, where, why, and how." Who leads the bereavement support groups? What are bereavement support groups? When and where are they held? Why would someone want to attend? How do the groups help?

Design the brochure so that interested parties do not have to search for information. The main items are who offers it, how much it costs, and where to call to get information. To keep the brochure current, avoid identifying the person who leads the group by name. Otherwise it will have to be reprinted each time there is a change in personnel; or if it is not reprinted, names will have to be crossed out or explanations made that the person advertised as the facilitator is no longer conducting the groups.

Brochures that fit into legal-size envelopes (4⅛ in. by 9½ in.) are the easiest to handle and mail. They display well if left in an agency's or doctor's office. Keep them to one or two pages. Stick to the essentials. One thickness printed on both sides should be enough. If more space is wanted, do not go over two folds, which gives six sides. This kind of brochure can be printed on letter-size paper, and when folded in three it fits into a legal-size envelope. The bereaved do not want to search through a wordy proclamation to find out what can be done for them, who can do it, and where they can go to get it done.

Use a logo and one color for the brochure and other printed handouts. Your color and logo design will identify bereavement support for those who attend the meetings and those who refer. A light-colored paper in a shade of yellow, green, or blue becomes known as the organization's trademark when it is used consistently. Black print stands out well against a light color and is easy to read. Make it even easier on the reader by printing the letters larger than standard typewriter print.

Brochures need to be put to work. Distribute them as widely as you can. Hospital social service departments need a good supply, as do home health agency nurses and social workers. Distribute them to churches, funeral directors, doctors' offices, attorneys, condominium associations, mobile home park managers, libraries, mental health centers, social workers, psychiatrists and psychologists in private practice, insurance agents, the chamber of commerce, schools, and anyplace else that will accept and display them. The bereaved are everywhere (Schiff, 1986). Keep each place supplied. Check every 2 to 3 months to see if more brochures are needed. The places that use the most are generally the best referral sources. Furnish them with one-time handouts on special events and additional materials that give helpful information on bereavement.

Yellow Pages

A listing in the telephone directory is essential to the success of any program and is a necessary cost of doing business. If a voluntary organization providing bereavement services has no funds, perhaps a sponsor can be found that will pay for listings in the white and yellow pages of the telephone book. If an organization provides services in several communities, each municipality's telephone directory will need to include the bereavement program's telephone number. If the service provider can only afford one line in the yellow pages, make sure that line is descriptive. The name listed must give an indication of what the organization does. Do not say "Central City Services"; say "Central City Bereavement Services."

If the organization can afford it, more elaborate advertising is available in the yellow pages. A separate ad can be purchased, color can be added, or a box giving descriptive information can be placed in the alphabetical listings.

Testimonials

Testimonials register in the subconscious. People become aware of what they have heard or read later on, when they need the service. In the pain of grief they may vaguely remember hearing that someone had recommended support groups for the bereaved.

Testimonials are short statements of gratitude, recommendations, explanations of how support groups have helped, or expressions of an individual's success achieved through the help of a bereavement group. Testimonials can come from the bereaved, from professionals, from experts, from well-known people in the community, or from anyone who has benefitted from a bereavement support group.

Testimonials are used in speeches, pamphlets, newsletters, flyers, brochures, and in information given to the media. They can be verbal or written. They can carry the name of the person attesting to the value of the support groups or can be anonymous. If the person's name is used, make sure that you have permission. If the name is not used, a description of the person is preferable to no identification. The words of appreciation might be followed by, "Widow, age 35, 3 children living at home," or "Widower, age 80, living alone." This personalizes the testimonial and lets the reader or listener identify who it was that found the service helpful. If the person sounds like someone who is like themselves, they are more likely to pay attention to the testimonial.

Proclamations

Every year there is at least one day or event that is worthy of a proclamation by city or county officials (Widowed Persons, 1987). None of these city or county managers is going to spontaneously declare a special day for the bereaved or honor an organization that has been providing services to the community. They may respond, however, if prompted by a request and an explanation of why a proclamation should be issued. Here are some ideas for proclamations:

- Volunteer week
- Anniversary of the organization
- The 1,000th person served
- Expansion of services

Check the library for existing officially sanctioned days, weeks, or months, and see if any of these national declarations apply to what the organization offers. Congress has been busy. There is not a month and there is hardly a day that has not been named for something or somebody. Ask for a local proclamation that honors what the bereavement support agency does along with the already-recognized day, week, or month. Have photographs or subjects for photographs available. Someone must also be available to accept the proclamation and say a few words.

Speeches

Let clubs and organizations in the community know that speakers are available to address their members. Make churches, government organizations, institutions, and social service and health care agencies aware that speakers are ready and willing to talk about bereavement services (Walterman, 1984).

Develop a speakers bureau by enlisting staff, volunteers, and satisfied customers. Determine what groups they are comfortable addressing and when and where they are willing to speak. Make sure they have the facts, and train them for their speaking engagements. Give each speaker a packet that includes handouts, information, interesting tidbits, testimonials, and a suggested speech outline. Assign a mentor to each new speaker. The neophyte speaker will first listen to the pro's presentation, then assist in a presentation, and finally make the speech while the mentor attends and monitors the performance. Recognize each speaker with a thank you, a listing of the speaking engagement in the newsletter, and special recognition for making an important contribution to the program. Speakers can receive points for each speech they make, with a gift, flower, pin, plaque, or some other small tangible item after each ten (or other number) of speeches.

Speeches not only spread the message throughout the community but often present opportunities for additional publicity for the bereavement support groups. Organizations use the media to announce who their speaker will be. Sometimes an editor will become interested in the topic and send a reporter to cover the meeting.

Bringing in popular or nationally known speakers is great publicity as well as a public service. Such speakers are usually high-priced, but their expenses can be covered if there is good advertising and a fee is charged those who attend. If continuing education credits are given for licensed personnel who work in the bereavement field, there will be an additional population eager to be present at the presentation. The local media will want to report on the distinguished visitor's speech and will give publicity to the sponsoring group. But do not rely on the media to give the desired publicity. Be prepared with an advertising campaign so that there will be a good crowd. Such an event takes a great deal of time and work. Do not undertake it unless there are people who are willing to do what is necessary to carry the project through to a successful completion.

Paid Advertising

Paid advertising is effective but can be expensive. A community college found that the adult education courses they offered had few students if it relied on the course catalog as the sole means of publicity. More students, sometimes even too many, showed up for classes that were listed in a weekly newspaper column on college activities. An excellent response also occurred when the courses were advertised in the local newspapers. Several ads over a period of time, combined with a mailing, proved the most productive. Advertising combined with other approaches, such as brochures, posted announcements, direct mailings, and newspaper features, brings the best results.

Advertising that catches the eye and calls for a commitment is the best. Displays larger than business-card size, which include information on bereavement support groups and ask interested parties to call or send in the ad with their names, addresses, and telephone numbers when they make reservations, induce the bereaved to plan ahead and can be an incentive for them to follow through. This format also gives the facilitator an idea of how many are coming.

If the organization uses paid advertising, it can also experiment with the location of the ad in the newspaper. Some programs routinely place their ads on the obituary page on Sundays.

Newsletters

Newsletters take time and ability. The person responsible for putting out the newsletter usually ends up doing most of the writing, coming up with the majority of the ideas, and having to harass contributors for their copy. If such a dedicated and able person can be found, a newsletter is a good way to generate publicity (Munneke, Foster, & Stombaugh, 1986).

Newsletters can be used for announcements; for giving recognition; to ask for help; to dramatize the service; to provide information, education, testimonials, and inspiration; and for promotion of the program. Anybody associated with the organization will be interested in the newsletter and want to read it. If the newsletter is employee based, it will meet a need and have readers who are already interested. As an internal organ, a newsletter is a nice thing, but as such does not answer the organization's need for publicity.

Because the newsletter is about the agency, updates on what is happening and what has been contributed by others are legitimately included. Profiles of staff members and their responsibilities are interesting to readers outside the organization. Think of the newsletter as a form of advertising, and design it to appeal to the general public. Avoid in-jokes and obscure references to the agency's employees. Always include an educational item about grief and grief services. It may be the results of research, information gleaned while attending conferences or workshops, statistics about the people served by the organization, or an item from a book or article. An inspirational piece is also appropriate. It can be a quote, saying, poem, report on progress of a bereaved person (with permission given to do so), or a note on what has been helpful to the bereaved. Now and then, offer to send out written information on topics of interest to the bereaved and those involved with them or copies of the living will. The requests for further information will give an indication of who is reading the newsletter.

A newsletter should be long enough to be more than a flyer, but not so long that it is too much for busy people to read within a short period. A newsletter comprising two to four 8½ in. by 11 in. sheets seems about right.

Decide how often the newsletter will be published. Do you have enough time and information to bring it out monthly? Will it be bimonthly, quarterly, or yearly? However often it is printed, the newsletter should be consistent in its appearance. It should arrive at the expected time and display the agency's logo and color, as they appear on all its public information. Prominently display the name and telephone number of the organization, indicating who should be called with referrals or for more information. Never leave any doubt as to the organization's purpose. Always include information on the location and number of bereavement support groups.

Will the newsletter carry advertising? Will a few sponsors be found to underwrite the costs of printing and mailing? Will it be professionally printed or run off on the organization's copying machine? Will there be pictures and illustrations? Give all these points some thought before undertaking a newsletter.

Send the newsletter to staff members and supporters, all past and present participants in bereavement support groups, churches, newspapers, housing complexes, health care facilities and agencies, social service organizations, libraries, schools, funeral homes, and any other person or agency with which there has been contact. Keep the mailing list up-to-date by asking that those who receive the newsletter send in a notice or call if they desire to continue their subscription. Whenever possible, add new people and places to the mailing list.

Yearly Calendar

When certain events are offered at regular intervals, people look forward to them. A hospice that planned spring and fall closed-end bereavement support groups for the widowed became well known in the community for providing that service. The bereaved counted on this and told others about it. If they had had a yearly calendar, they could have planned their time around these groups.

The yearly calendar should be distributed throughout the community to anybody and everybody who might have contact with the bereaved. It would include ongoing as well as one-time-only events. Although a yearly calendar does not preclude adding new events and services, it is never a good idea to drop anything that is printed on the calendar. If that is done the calendar becomes useless. People will no longer see it as accurate, will not use it for their own reference, and will not tell others about upcoming events that might be of interest to them. A yearly calendar is good publicity because it allows people to plan ahead and to make specific referrals for needed services; it displays the agency's activities and services and is a vivid example of the organization's viability. On slow news days a reporter can always refer to it to find a story.

Do not think about publishing a yearly calendar for mass distribution if the organization and its personnel are in a state of flux. Do publish one if the support groups and employees are well established and annual events and programs take place regularly. It is a quick and easy reference that usually produces increased referrals. If the calendar is printed so that professionals who work with the bereaved can use it for their own appointments, it will be a particularly easy guide for them and an incentive to let the bereaved know about the support groups that are available to help them.

Trade, Home, and Senior Citizen Shows

Rent a booth at any appropriate trade show. Enlist graduates of bereavement support groups to be available for questions or to distribute newsletters, brochures, flyers, schedules, or small favors such as pencils, note pads, or key rings with the organization's name, logo, and telephone number.

The best advertising is always word-of-mouth. These are opportunities for satisfied customers to let interested people know about the benefits of bereavement support groups.

If the bereavement support groups are part of a health care agency such as a hospital or hospice, information can be distributed at health fairs, while blood pressures are taken or other health-related information is made available to the public.

County fairs also have areas where entrepreneurs exhibit items for sale, demonstration, or publicity. Bereavement support groups can be advertised there, just as they are at trade shows.

Courses

Some people who will not attend support groups will go to educational events. They will learn about grief, gain from the knowledge, and tell others about the organization.

Courses on the grief process and the use of groups to assist the bereaved are of interest to professionals in the community. They will attend for the added expertise, will become more aware of the benefits of groups for the bereaved, and will be more likely to refer the grief stricken for group support. If continuing education units are offered, a fee can be charged; professionals will turn out so that they can accrue continuing education units. Invite mental health and other health professionals to participate in training sessions, seminars, workshops, and classes. Include estate planners, insurance agents, teachers, law enforcement personnel, and lawyers as well.

Seminars can be planned for the bereaved and for the general public. Training sessions can be tailored exclusively for professionals. Advertising the seminars and courses so that the information reaches targeted groups is essential to get people to attend. The only way to avoid having to handle such publicity is to get someone else to do it. That can be done if the presentation is made to a captive audience, such as the nursing staff at a hospital, a luncheon or dinner meeting, or a church congregation, to name a few possibilities. Sometimes another organization will sponsor a training session and advertise the offering to its constituents. Some professional groups may do this: funeral directors, the National Association of Social Workers, or ministerial or nursing associations. Seminars and training sessions can be taught through the auspices of a local college. In that case the course will be listed in the college's catalog. The college then takes responsibility for the distribution of the course catalog in the community.

The following are some possible topics for seminars:

Life changes after the death of a spouse.
The many aspects of grief.

Grief survival.
How to help yourself through grief.
Parental grief.
Children's grief.

Training sessions for professionals can include any information that is helpful to those who are bereaved and instructive to the general public but should cover additional topics as well:

Complicated grief.
The tasks of the bereaved.
Symptoms of grief.
Community resources that are available to assist the bereaved.
Different responses to grief.
Techniques for alleviating grief.
An understanding of attitudes toward death.
Care for the caregivers.
Normal grief reactions.
Disenfranchised grief; mourning deaths due to AIDS, suicide, or the death penalty.

Information Packets

Do not overwhelm people with information. Give them what they request. People throw away what they do not want and are irritated if they have to wade through several brochures and sheets of paper to get to what interests them. Consequently, informational packets that contain comprehensive information about bereavement support groups should not be given to everyone. If there is a request for specific information, such as the support group schedule, a telephone number, or an address, it is usually best to give that, rather than burden people with a lot of what they do not want or need. Once information packets are available they tend to be used indiscriminately. They should not be. They are best distributed at training sessions, to professionals and media personnel, and at trade shows. Informational packets are impressive and project order and competence. If they look good they make the organization look good. But they do not suffice as a response to people who are looking for help and need specific information.

Outreach

The most successful bereavement support programs incorporate some type of outreach. The stress of grief often makes it difficult for the bereaved to reach out and find the help they need. They do not know that help is available or indeed that there *is* anything that can help them. And even if they do, they are too disorganized and distressed to seek the help: They need help to get help.

Cards and Letters   Hospice agencies, the Widowed Persons Service, and many funeral homes use an orderly process to enlist the participation of the bereaved in support services that are designed to help them. It is called *outreach*. It includes writing, telephoning, and face-to-face contact. Outreach usually starts with cards or letters and moves to the desired goal of a personal encounter.

Some of the bereaved will respond to written invitations to attend bereavement support groups. The arrival of a card or letter inviting them to participate may be just what they are looking for, at the time they are looking for it, and will be all the encouragement they need. On the other hand, the first invitation may be ignored. Recipients may decide it is not for them; they feel too bad; they do not feel that bad; or they are too busy. The program may have to correspond with them two or three times over months or years before they decide that a support group might be something that they should try.

If the bereaved have had prior dealings with the organization or have been referred by someone they know and trust, they are more likely to respond to an invitation than if they wonder how their names were obtained. After experiencing a traumatic loss and the concomitant overwhelming feelings of despair, the bereaved are less confident and more suspicious. They are unsure of themselves and may find it difficult to go to a new place alone.

Telephone Calls   Because many of the bereaved who have not responded to the cards and letters can be helped through bereavement support groups, the next step is a telephone call. The correspondence can indicate that if the recipients do not call, they will be called. The card or letter introduces the service; the caller follows up with a personal invitation. The call can come from an employee of the organization, since professionals tend to be trusted, but it is more effective if it can be placed by someone who has suffered a similar loss and has a genuine conviction that support groups are helpful to the bereaved. The person who has been through what the newly bereaved person is going through will have more credibility and will be more convincing. Nevertheless, the bereaved will not necessarily jump at participating in a group. They may continue to be afraid to talk about their grief in a room full of strangers.

Face-to-Face Visits   The bereaved person may agree to a one-to-one meeting. This does not guarantee that they will then have all their fears allayed and readily attend a bereavement support group, even though a face-to-face visit instills confidence. If the visitor has been bereaved, that will give the newly bereaved hope for their own survival and convince them to go to a bereavement support group. If the outreach person will accompany them, that may be the last little bit of encouragement they need to decide to give it a try.

Extra Help

If bereavement support groups can be held at convenient locations, in well-lighted, safe areas with adequate parking, it will help attendance. The more accessible the meetings are, the more people will avail themselves of them. Location is important. So is time. Many of the elderly no longer drive at night. Some have given up driving altogether. Some never learned. No one wants to go to a new group in an unfamiliar part of town. Offer bereavement support groups in different locations throughout the community, either concurrently or alternately. Keep track of which times and places promote the best attendance. Practically any place can be a bereavement support group location. Banks, churches, community centers, libraries, social and health agencies, and hospitals all have conference rooms that they may be willing to lend to the group at no cost for an hour or two, once a week. Just make sure that the space is reasonably easy to find, has adequate lighting and seating, good temperature control, and that the group will not be disturbed. Privacy is essential.

Those who do not drive or are reluctant to venture out will have to have transportation arranged for them if they are to be persuaded to attend the group. Volunteers or other members of the group may be available to drive them. If arrangements can be made with other bereavement support group members, there will be added benefits in that the new arrival will have an escort to the group and a friendship may develop.

Many individuals who plan to go to a bereavement support group, get to the parking lot, and are unable to get themselves through the door and into the meeting. Have someone outside the door to greet newcomers and help them into the session. The most self-assured can be humbled by grief and fearful of facing the unknown. The pain of loss, coupled with anxiety over talking about it with others, is a combination that can immobilize. As much as people want help for their pain, they also want to avoid the pain. Stalemate results. They frequently find that the promise of help in an unknown situation is less inviting, and they return home defeated and frustrated. Thus providing a companion or giving transportation are effective aids. For attendees who do not make their needs known, but who just show up, having greeters available to shepherd them gently into the room may be the initial reassurance that enables them to get the help they need.

Joint Ventures

Outreach can be accomplished through the auspices of other agencies. If the organization's bereavement support groups are underattended by certain groups of the bereaved, such as AIDS survivors or parents of children who were lost to SIDS (Sudden Infant Death Syndrome), consider working in cooperation with an AIDS organization or the health department. To reach the mourners, collaborate with the agency or organization that has had contact with the deceased and their families. Hold bereavement groups in their facilities. Ask them to sponsor the groups, or bring in a cofacilitator from that agency. Rely on them to do the needed outreach.

As we have discussed, the more the community knows about the agency's services, the more the services will be used. Publicity is never a one-shot deal. It has to be continuous, so that the bereaved will know what is available at the time they need it. Fortunately, there are many ways to keep the provider's name and services in the public eye. The use of the mass media, brochures, newsletters, and paid advertising can generate constant and far-reaching publicity. Offering services to the public in times of need or catastrophe or providing educational events will enhance the agency's reputation as a knowledgeable and compassionate organization. Informative promotions regularly generated will result in a strong bereavement support group program.

Chapter 4

Setting Up a Bereavement Support Group

If a group of bereaved people are recruited and put in a room together, they may find ways to support one another, but the struggle will soon get old. People who find themselves responsive to each other will pair off, and others will simply disappear unless a natural leader emerges who can facilitate the group. It is no accident that support groups have leaders, rules, procedures, and expectations. Such order is necessary if the group is to function and prosper.

THE FACILITATOR

The facilitator may be a professional and an employee, and may also be one who has suffered a traumatic loss. The facilitator may be a volunteer—someone who is trained in leading groups. The facilitator may also be someone with a natural talent that developed as the person attended support groups and who works as a cofacilitator or with professional back-up.

Do not underestimate the importance of a group facilitator. Several qualities must combine if the person or persons are to do the job effectively. Coleaders can complement each other, each doing what he or she does best. Effective bereavement support group facilitators will have enough time; will be able to give attention to detail; and will demonstrate compassion, understanding, and empathy. They will be organized, flexible, knowledgeable, accepting, patient, and creative. They will be good listeners, always willing to learn.

Organizational Skills

Time   A good facilitator must take the time to be with the group. The participants must never feel as though they are being hurried or that the leader needs to rush them along because of important upcoming appointments or projects.

The skillful group facilitator understands that it takes as much time to prepare for the group as to conduct the group. It takes time to recruit and screen attendees; to plan the meetings; to prepare handouts; to follow up on participants who are upset or who do not attend a meeting; to write notes; to set up the room; to prepare name tags, refreshments, and attendance lists; to find resources in the community for the bereaved who need more than group support; to communicate with others involved in helping the support group members; and to assemble supplies. Even if much of this work can be delegated to support staff or volunteers, the group leader bears the ultimate responsibility for seeing that it is done. Anybody leading a group has to have talent for more than group work (Masson & Jacobs, 1980).

Recruitment and Screening   The facilitator determines who will be recruited for the support group. Will the group be designed for anyone in grief or for a select group, such as widows, parents, adolescents? Will recruitment be through advertising, mailings, outreach, or all of the above? Will recruitment stop once the group is started, or will it be continuous?

Support groups cannot help everyone. Although there is great tolerance for diversity in self-help groups, there has to be some commonalty among the members. Neither can one person's problems monopolize all the sessions. The facilitator will decide what kinds of losses can be helped in a specific group and set limits as to how long ago the loss shall have occurred; decide whether relatives may attend the same group and whether a prospective group member will be able to benefit from the group process.

Plan the Meetings   How long will each session be? Will the support group meet a specified number of times, or will it be ongoing? How often will it meet, and where? What is the agenda? How will the program meet the needs of the participants? Who will do what in each meeting (Madara & Meese, 1986)?

Prepare Handouts   People who attend bereavement support groups are emotional. With high emotion comes anxiety. When anxiety is high, hearing is impaired: Words and messages are missed or misinterpreted. There is too much to take in at once. Handouts are effective for that reason. The bereaved can read a handout as often as they need to until they grasp how they can use the information for themselves.

Not all participants will benefit from handouts, as everyone learns through different channels. Some learn best by example or by verbal instructions. For them the handouts will be a backup for information they are receiving in other ways. Those who learn most readily from the written word will use what they hear and see in the group as confirmation of what they read.

But no matter how the participants learn and no matter how emotional they are, they will appreciate handouts, which are symbols of the help proffered them and of hope and caring. Handouts are something tangible they can take with them when they leave the group.

Not just any handout will do. The materials should be brief and specifically helpful. Time-limited, closed-end groups use handouts most effectively when they coincide with the discussion topics and are progressively explanatory. Handouts may be educational, inspirational, or interpretive—something with which the bereaved can identify, or a story of how people in grief dealt constructively with their loss.

Handouts can be written by the group leader, but that is not necessary inasmuch as so much helpful material is already available. In either instance, it takes time to prepare the handouts or get permission from the authors to make and distribute copies. Have an ample supply of each handout available so that no participant will be slighted.

Follow Up on Participants   When participants are visibly upset when they leave the group meeting, it is up to the leader to telephone them to determine if more help is needed. Although the participants may be in no danger and the emotional upset may be momentary, they will appreciate having the facilitator call to find out how they are. In some instances the call may save a life.

One of the therapeutic aspects of a bereavement support group is the bonding of the group members. The facilitator is obliged to check on attendees who do not show up because that is one of the leader's responsibilities to the group. Additionally, the facilitator has to demonstrate that all group members are involved with each group member. There is a mutual caring to be expressed. When someone who has attended the support group drops out, it is important to show that caring by calling and reporting back to the group. Showing that there is concern about what happens to each group member shows that there is concern about every group member (Nudell, 1987). The facilitator should also call absent participants to gather information about the group. For example, some people will leave because they do not like being in a group or because they find something about the group offensive. Only through checking with those who attended will the facilitator learn what helps, what does not, and who is best able to use the group.

Write Notes Documentation is necessary. At a minimum there should be a record of the names, addresses, and telephone numbers of all bereavement group participants. If the individuals have been customers of the organization that sponsors the bereavement support group, a note of the survivors' attendance will be needed for the agency's files.

The facilitator should keep notes on what was discussed in each meeting and what worked. Participants frequently bring in information, helpful articles, and meaningful poems. They request that certain topics be added to the group's agenda. The leader must research community resources that are available to meet the needs of the participants. All such information is not only presented to the bereavement group members but is also kept for future groups.

Set Up the Room To better accommodate the participants, several meeting places in various areas in the community may be used. That means assembling the materials so that they can be transported from place to place. The facilitator needs a correct attendance list for each venue, handouts, tissues, name tags, and refreshments. It is helpful if each meeting place has a storage area that the leader can use to avoid having always to carry materials from place to place. If the meeting place is a multipurpose room, the chairs will probably have to be rearranged. There are name tags to prepare and refreshments to set out. Handouts must be collated and made ready. Someone should be available to greet the newcomers and give special assistance to anyone who walks out or becomes overwhelmed with grief. An assistant is invaluable. If a volunteer can be found to fill this position, he or she will feel very much needed.

Unfortunately, when bereavement support groups are conducted throughout the community in borrowed places, it is difficult to find meeting rooms that have all the desired amenities, such as a comfortable temperature, good chairs, a table to sit around, a kitchen for refreshments, rest rooms that are easy to find, and a counter for signing in and for displaying the handouts.

Attention to Detail and Organization Bereavement support groups are run for the benefit of the bereaved. Everything that can reasonably be done to increase their enjoyment, boost their learning, enhance their self-esteem, augment their confidence, enlarge their world, and deal with their pain, and in short, to make them feel more comfortable and hopeful, should be done. All of this is part of what is expected to happen in bereavement support groups.

Since the goals of bereavement support groups are focused on the bereaved and devoted to a good outcome for each of them, the facilitator cannot leave what happens to chance. Minute, seemingly inconsequential trifles can cause the bereaved person to feel unwelcome, upset, or hurt. Not every misunderstanding or misperception can be avoided. Facilitators can, however, pay attention to detail so that problems may be forestalled. Some of the bereaved have said such things as the following:

"No one comforted me when I cried."

"I tried to say something but no one paid any attention to me."

"I asked to be notified of the meetings but did not hear."

"My name did not get on the mailing list."

"The leader greeted everyone at the door but me."

"When I left before the meeting was over no one asked why."

"There were never enough handouts to go around."

"I heard others planning social events, and I was not invited."

"They acted like my problem wasn't important."

"When my car broke down no one offered me a ride, although others had transportation arranged for them."

"The leader kept calling me by my real name rather than the nickname I preferred."

"I was forced to talk when I did not want to."

"I got sick, but no one asked how I was when I returned to the group."

"The directions to the meeting place were confusing to me. I got lost and was late for the first three sessions. A map would have helped."

"The resource list did not include places a single woman can go for socializing. I kept asking about that."

"I wanted more bereavement support than the six sessions offered, and I was not told what else was available."

"There were no evening sessions offered, and I could not get off work to attend. I always asked for an evening session, but if any were ever scheduled, I was not told about them."

"I can't drink caffeine or eat sugar. They always had coffee and cookies for refreshments."

"My name was misspelled on my name tag."

"When the names and telephone numbers were given out, I found I had the wrong number for the person I tried to call. After that I gave up and did not try to call anyone else."

"Nobody complained about the temperature, but I was always too hot."

"I didn't get to the first series of bereavement support that I wanted to go to, as I expected someone to call me back after I phoned in my reservation."

Attention to detail means that everyone feels as though they had received a personal invitation and a personal welcome and that everything possible was done to make them feel they were in the right place. Everybody cannot have everything they want, but all should feel as though they are heard and considered. Names spelled wrong, incorrect telephone numbers, a disorganized presentation, inadequate supplies, and an uncomfortable setting are irritating. The bereaved already feel that nothing is going right for them. When they go someplace for help, they want to think that that place is secure enough to give them some badly needed stability.

Objective Skills

Leaders cannot know everything. No leader can know what all participants are feeling, how they will manage, and what will help them. In fact, the more knowledgeable the group facilitators are, the more they realize how much they do not know. Nevertheless, facilitators must have some specific kinds of knowledge if they are to be successful support group leaders.

Knowledge of Bereavement

The grief process   Bereavement group facilitators are obligated to have an understanding of the grief process, the symptoms and complications of grief, and this culture's prevalent attitudes toward those in grief. Their awareness of the normal grief reaction—and the ability to convey to the bereaved that it *is* normal—is part of the reassurance and strength that they impart to the group participants. It gives them hope (Baldwin, 1993).

If the group's leaders have personal knowledge of traumatic loss, there can be an instant cohesiveness. However, these facilitators will have to be aware that their experiences are not everyone's experience. Personal knowledge must be tempered by the realization that each experience is unique and that feelings and reactions to loss are not good or bad, just different.

If the group leaders' knowledge comes from books, instruction, and talking with the bereaved, it is still valuable and useful. These facilitators can share what they have learned from others. There will be acceptance based on the leaders' efforts to gain knowledge and understanding and their ability to share what they have learned. They, like everyone else, cannot say what the bereaved ought to do, but they can convey how others have managed a particular situation. Sharing knowledge is different from giving advice. If the facilitators are sensitive and indicate that they know what they know because they listen to those who do know, the group members may give them their highest compliment, "You sound like one of us."

Different kinds of losses   Loss is loss; but losses cannot be compared, and some losses leave the bereaved in a high-risk category (Marvel, 1992). Disenfranchised grief is different from normal grief because the losses are not openly acknowledged or publicly mourned. Perinatal, drug-related, self-inflicted, and AIDS deaths are oppressive to deal with because guilt, shame, and anger are so much a part of the emotions of mourning. Deaths caused by a family member's accident, abuse, or murder are complicated by fear and blame. Deaths that occur in mental institutions, drug rehabilitation centers, jail, or in the homes of paramours cause confusion for those in the bereaved person's support system. They do not know what to say, so they ignore it. Tenuous relationships, as when the bereaved person is mourning the death of an ex-spouse or lover, a co-worker, a patient, client, or customer, do not routinely elicit the acknowledgement and concern that the bereaved need.

People killed while committing a crime, who are murdered by spouses acting in self-defense, or who survive a murder-suicide pact leave mourners with ambivalent feelings and culturally unsanctioned grief. They do not know what they feel or where to go for help.

Bereavement support group facilitators need to understand the complicated aspects of these deaths and the turbulent feelings of the survivors. The group leaders will have to decide whether they can profit from attending a group, whether they need a specialized group, or if they can benefit most from individual support.

Knowledge of Group Processes

Group dynamics   The facilitators' knowledge of group dynamics can make or break a group. The leaders' responsibility is to the group, which is the treatment tool. Problems are solved in the group and by the group members. If the facilitators do not select the right combination of people or do not keep the group working as a collection of people addressing similar problems, the participants will become frustrated and disenchanted. Facilitators must not do one-to-one therapy in the group, include people who cannot work in a group, select participants whose problems are overwhelming or inappropriate for a bereavement support group, or let group members with the idea that their way is the only way dominate. The facilitators must maintain a nonthreatening, nonjudgmental environment if the group is to be a functioning support group.

The group dynamics differ in each group and from one type of group to another. Leading a support group is not the same as leading groups geared to insight or behavioral or personality changes, nor is it like working with groups set up to help participants adapt to the norms of the larger community. A bereavement support group is a self-help group. Education, reassurance, management of stress, understanding, the release of emotions, acceptance, tolerance, self-affirmation, interpretation, reinforcement, and clarification are all used in support groups (Sweeney, 1991). The facilitators serve as guides. The group members are encouraged and assisted in helping one another. The group leaders and the members are dealing with a crisis. People in crisis need support (Van Ornum & Mordock, 1990) that helps them marshal their thoughts and feelings so that they can implement effective coping strategies and better manage the exigencies of their daily lives.

Bereavement support groups facilitators must recognize the vulnerability of the participants and actively protect them. Bereavement support group members cannot be expected to establish group norms and enforce group rules. The group leaders must see that as their job, particularly in closed-end groups where the sanctions of the group do not have time to become fully established. Leadership must be firm but flexible.

Protecting individual group members from embarrassment, from revealing too much too soon, from attack by others, or from the good intentions of participants who want to take over does not mean that group members are spared their own emotions and distresses. These are encouraged and accepted.

It is necessary for the facilitators to identify and manage anxiety so that it is not artificially elicited. Group members should not have to get anxious about seating arrangements, starting and stopping times, about what will happen to a particularly disturbed group member, or about any personal problems or limitations that the leaders might have. In contrast, anxiety related to bereavement is expected and its expression encouraged.

Therapeutic-group norms   The group facilitators need to have a clear knowledge of group norms. Group members should be made aware of them before they enter the group and have them reinforced during the first meeting and as needed thereafter. Norms are the rules of the group. Norms for a bereavement support group will differ from the norms for a group of juvenile delinquents. The facilitators will know what they are, why the norms are important for the group, and how to sustain them. The group members look to the leaders for direction; it should be clearly and consistently given (Yalom, 1985).

Knowledge of Psychodynamics

Psychopathology Knowledge of behavior that is dangerously self-destructive and requires specialized attention and care is essential. The facilitators will need to know when bereavement is complicated by clinical depression, when anxiety becomes a panic attack or a phobia, when para-normal contacts with the deceased are hallucinations, and when despair is so intense that thoughts of dying turn to plans for suicide. These problems cannot be addressed in a support group. Treatment by mental health specialists is needed.

Techniques to teach group interactions Knowledgeable group leaders know how to encourage interaction among group members so that communication takes place without its being directed toward the facilitators. The group members work with each other, not through the leaders. The facilitators also have positive and effective techniques for keeping the group moving and on task and for making sure that learning takes place in a constructive and affirmative manner. The leaders emphasize points through subtle intervention; they reinforce meaningful points and ideas by giving verbal and nonverbal indications of approval that underline what the participants said.

Nonverbal communication Knowing facilitators understand body language, and if they cannot interpret the posture, gesture, or look, they know to ask. Nonverbal communication is more powerful than the spoken word. People may forget what is said but will not forget how it is said. It is helpful to have cofacilitators so that there is more opportunity to observe and pick up on the unspoken messages (Corey, 1990).

Awareness The group facilitators are aware of their roles as leaders and knowledgeable about how that function influences the group norms. What the facilitators do or do not do impinges on the tone of the group and the behavior of the participants. The facilitators' awareness of their own actions and attitudes is crucial, as the participants look to them for direction. The bereaved may not have had prior experience in support groups and thus may tune in to the leaders' verbal and nonverbal messages as indications of what is and is not done. If the group is not performing as desired, the leaders need to know how their words and actions contribute to this. They also need to know when they can take credit for a group that operates well.

Knowledge of Community: Resources

It will become apparent that some of the participants will have to be referred elsewhere or will need supplementary assistance. The facilitators will be able to do this because of their knowledge of the community resources that can provide the help the individuals need. A working relationship with those providers will ease the way for the bereaved.

Knowledge of Self: Personal Versus Professional Concerns

Bereavement group facilitators are expected to have feelings but are not expected to use the group to help themselves work through these feelings. A personal experience with loss and grief is helpful for empathizing with the group members, but unhelpful if the grief has not been resolved to the point that the leaders can maintain the role of facilitator.

The leaders cannot totally divorce themselves from all feelings and concerns. They will, however, need a professional knowledge and ability to keep from becoming overinvolved in the lives of the group members or taking group members' actions and reactions personally. If a group member leaves the group it is a professional, not a personal, concern. If participants complain about the agenda or suggest changes, the matter is weighed professionally, not taken as personal criticism. The group leaders' knowledge of professional behavior is of paramount importance. They must understand when to intercede and when to retreat. They do not try to help the lonely group members become socialized by taking them out but suggest possibilities that they can pursue on their own or with other group members.

It is the facilitators' job to deal tactfully and professionally with absences, lateness, and disruptive behavior, never taking personal affront at behaviors that work against group cohesiveness and frustrate the leaders' desire for the uninterrupted forward movement of the agenda.

Subjective Skills

Compassion, Understanding, Empathy, and Acceptance   The leaders may be volunteers or paid employees. In either case the bereavement support group members want to know that the facilitators are there because they care. The bereaved will identify more readily with someone who has been through an experience similar to theirs, but they will accept the professional who makes the effort to understand and who demonstrates empathy.

The bereaved will not accept leaders who have all the answers, do all the talking, are there only because it is their job assignment, or are conducting the group because of the attention and power it gives them.

Feeling sorry for the bereaved is not the same as feeling compassion, understanding, empathy, and acceptance (Wolfelt, 1989). Sympathy is belittling. It says to the bereaved that they are pitiful creatures who are unable to care for themselves. The bereaved appreciate concern but do not like feeling that they are not considered able. They have enough doubts of their own. They do not need a group leader who reinforces those doubts.

Being interested, hoping that all goes well for the group participants, and making every effort to help them achieve what they want are not the same as taking over for them, telling them what they should do, or doing for them what they can do for themselves. Helping the bereaved do what they must do validates them. Doing it for them diminishes them. Creating dependency is insulting and is not a compassionate action.

Flexibility and Patience   The group facilitators set the tone for the group. By action and words they let the participants know that it is all right to repeat the same story again and again, to have fears, and to feel disheartened. As they show their acceptance of one person in the group, they confirm their acceptance of all in the group. The leaders do not set a schedule for the recovery of the bereaved. They are patient. They let all the group members move at their own pace and in their own way.

Although the facilitators have a plan for the meeting, they are not rigid about it. If the bereaved have problems they want to discuss or if the group gets involved in another pressing topic, the agenda can be shelved. The participants can decide what they need to talk about, and the leaders can adjust accordingly.

Flexibility is needed in other areas as well. When meeting rooms are donated by others, flexibility may make the difference between a successful group and no group. The group may be locked out, the room occupied, or the meeting place uninhabitable. It takes flexibility to make the best of these bad situations and have a group meeting in a restaurant, on the lawn or the steps, in someone's home or an alternate room, or simply to speak briefly with the group members and call it a day. In other words, the best of plans can be thwarted. It takes flexibility, patience, and good humor to manage no matter what.

Good Listening Skills   Bereaved support group participants do not want a lecture. They want to talk with each other. They need facilitators to keep them on track, to keep one person from monopolizing all the sessions, and to carry out the administrative tasks that make it possible for the group to meet.

A good listener asks questions, clarifies issues, involves others in the discussion, and generalizes from specific reports. He or she knows when everyone has listened enough and it is time to summarize and move on. A good listener also picks up on problems that merit further deliberation and asks for suggestions from the group participants. This is a person who knows when to give direction, when to involve others, when to explain to the rest of the group why the speaker's problem needs further attention and time, recognizes when individuals need more help than they can get in a support group.

A good listener knows that when in doubt the best thing to do is to listen. A good listener does not rush in with solutions, interrupt when someone is talking, reassure prematurely, or tell the bereaved what they really mean.

Willingness to Learn   A good listener will learn. This listening and learning will make for more effective group facilitators. Those who are willing to learn will discover that learning occurs all the time. They will note that just when they think they have heard it all, they haven't, and just when they think they understand completely, someone will bring up a new angle. They will learn that there are no absolutes in the grief process; that all people do the best that they can; that the best help that can be given is the help the bereaved need when they need it; and that facilitators have to listen to learn what and when that is.

When the facilitators think they have learned a great deal about grieving, they will learn that they have not learned everything there is to know about the individual in grief.

Group facilitators who recognize that they will never know it all, and who approach each experience with each group member as a learning experience, will convey enthusiasm and interest. The support group participants will appreciate that.

Group facilitators who are willing to learn, and who recognize that there is always something to learn, will remain fresh and enjoy their work. They will not get stagnant and bored. Everyone will appreciate that.

Creativity   If one thing does not work, something else may. Being creative does not mean that one must be able to write poems or paint pictures. It means that one can approach old problems in new ways, keep an open mind, try new approaches, build on what works, and know how to make the best of a bad situation. Facilitating a bereavement group is never cut-and-dried. There may be an agenda and a routine, but there is seldom total predictability.

Fallibility   Group leaders do not have to be perfect and are cautioned against trying to appear infallible. The facilitators in bereavement support

groups are expected to be human, respond on a human level, be spontaneous, admit mistakes, ask for interpretation and suggestions from the
"experts," and be involved. Even though they are removed from the group
because they are leading it, they are part of the group because they have an
investment in good results.

SCREENING THE PARTICIPANTS

Not all bereavement group facilitators screen prospective participants.
There are ongoing groups that are open to anyone who has experienced the
death of a loved one. Of course, the criterion that the participants are
bereaved is in itself a form of screening in that it defines the support group
population.

Whether or not to screen depends on how specialized the group is to
be, on the availability of appropriate bereavement services, on how much
time the group facilitators have, and on the number of bereaved available to
make up a group.

Screening is sometimes not done in the belief that prospective group
members will screen themselves out if they feel the approach is not right for
them. Sometimes the number of available bereaved is limited to such an
extent that unless everyone is urged to attend, there will be no group. It
may also be assumed that if someone attends the bereavement group, and it
is apparent the individual has more problems than can be addressed there,
he or she can be referred to the appropriate treatment source.

Nevertheless, screening should be done and can be based on simple,
but useful, criteria.

Bereavement

The facilitator can accept anyone who is bereaved or can limit groups to
those bereaved because of the loss of a spouse, or a child, or a parent, or a
sibling, or any loss that is common enough that a number of people can be
recruited to form a support group.

Admittance into specialized bereavement support groups can be
further limited. There can be women- or men-only groups; groups comprising those who have lost a young child or experienced the sudden death of a
child; losses from violent death or accidental death. There may be groups
of young widows or widowers, military spouses or families, AIDS survivors,
children whose parents have died, or any configuration that meets the
special needs of a group of people who have experienced a similar loss.

Length of Bereavement

The facilitator may decide to screen out individuals whose loss was so
recent that they are still in a state of shock or may exclude the bereaved

whose loss occurred over five years ago because they can no longer identify with the pain of a recent loss. The bereaved who attend a support group before the reality of their loss has hit them end up going to another series at a later time because early on they were not ready to take in much of what was said and done. They were still numb. The bereaved who experienced their loss several years earlier may not have dealt with it either at the time of the loss or in the ensuing years; something may have occurred in their lives that now makes it necessary for them to face their delayed grief. When screening by length of bereavement, it is difficult to set absolute limits because of such individual needs. Therefore the guidelines should be flexible. It often works well to have a support group composed of people in different stages of grief. Those who have progressed are helps and role models for those who have farther to go.

Special Problems of Support Group Members

Some bereaved persons have problems that are so severe that they need individual assistance and direction. Their problems are so great that they overwhelm the support group members. Instead of working on their own problems, support group members get caught up in the major difficulties of a needy individual. In such a case the others will resent the fact that someone in the group needs so much help or that their problems seem inconsequential in comparison. They will see the support group as a place that does not meet their needs when what is really the case is that the support group cannot meet the needs of the person with many and complicated problems.

In some instances people with mental health problems can attend bereavement support groups concurrently with their other treatments. If that is to occur, the symptoms of their diagnoses must be under control. If you have doubts, get permission from the prospective group member and consult with his or her physician or counselor (American Psychiatric Association, 1987).

Depression   A diagnosis of depression is different from the grieving person's feelings of sadness. A clinical depression requires the help of a specialist and probably medication. Depressed people cannot be cheered up, feel they cannot do anything right, are down on themselves, feel empty, hopeless, helpless, and are irritable. The diagnosis may be major depression (acute), dysthymic disorder (chronic), atypical depression (persistent but not acute or chronic), or bipolar disorder (cyclical periods of depression, sometimes alternating with manic episodes). The bereaved with these diagnoses are able to attend a support group if the depression is controlled. If not controlled, their depression will be so debilitating that they will not be able to function as a group member. Their inability to respond to suggestions and encouragement will drag down the other group members.

Schizophrenia A person with schizophrenia needs psychiatric help and medication and, at times, will suffer a break with reality. They may be paranoid, hear voices, and misinterpret social cues. They may feel threatened in a support group and frighten the other participants.

Phobic or Panic Disorders Although anxiety does not preclude support group attendance, it is difficult for a person who is experiencing disabling anxiety to think of anything else when in the throes of an attack. Diagnosis of phobic or panic disorder means that the individual should be receiving counseling and may be taking medication. If the diagnosis is a post-traumatic stress disorder, the same recommendation applies. People with that disorder react to current events as they did during the past trauma. The flashbacks are so real that it is impossible for them to function in a group. Because these problems are relatively easy to control, the red flag is the diagnosis. Investigation may reveal that the symptoms are mild or nonexistent and will not interfere with support group functioning.

Dissociative Disorders The bereaved who dissociate are not appropriate for a bereavement support group because they forget, change personalities, or are unable to recall elementary personal information. Diagnosis of multiple personality disorder or psychogenic fugue or amnesia should prompt a contact with the individual's counselor.

Manic States If prospective group participants have cyclothymic or bipolar disorder, manic, check with the individual's physician. They need medication to moderate their hyperactivity, pressure of speech, flight of ideas, racing thoughts, and excessive sensitivity to stimuli. In a manic state, they cannot attend to one thought or theme and will take over the group and destroy the process for others.

Substance Use Disorders Abuse of alcohol or other legal or illegal drugs needs to be treated before individuals involve themselves with a bereavement group. Unless abuse of mind-altering substances is controlled, the group experience will be lost on them and will be ruined for the others in the group.

Other Debilitating Problems Overwhelming health problems or problems with daily living may so distress and preoccupy the bereaved that they are unable to deal with their grief. They will also distress and preoccupy the bereavement group members to the point that nothing will be achieved and everyone will become frustrated. People who are suffering morbid grief reactions (see chapter 1, complicated grief), who have personal health problems that take priority, relationship problems that are destructive, or insubstantial living arrangements with constant crisis, need one-to-one help and assistance with material necessities; they cannot productively involve themselves in a bereavement support group. This modality will not help them and will jeopardize the function of the group and the stability of the participants.

Referrals   The facilitators will want to offer help to the bereaved who approach them about support groups, but who need more. Resources in the community can provide assistance.

Mental health problems   Refer to community mental health centers if money is limited or to psychotherapists in private practice if insurance or finances are available.

Substance abuse   Refer to Alcoholics or Narcotics Anonymous, community mental health drug rehabilitation programs, or inpatient treatment centers.

Health problems   Refer to appropriate medical specialists or to a county or community health care agency.

Relationship problems   Refer to the community mental health center, a family counseling center, or counselors in private practice.

Financial problems   Refer to the state health and economic services agency for food stamps, to the Social Security Administration for Supplemental Security Income (SSI) and Medicaid, to county welfare or local charitable organizations for food, shelter, and clothing, and to the housing authority for low-cost housing.

Exploitation, abuse, neglect   Report all instances of exploitation, abuse, or neglect to the toll-free abuse line.

Screening Checklist

A screening checklist, like the one shown in Table 4.1, helps the interviewer to organize the collection of information so that judgments can be based on facts rather than impressions.

The secret of a screening session is the conversational approach. All of the questions can be asked during the course of the interview without slavishly going down the screening checklist. Taking notes is acceptable; coldly addressing personal problems while completing a form is not. In the

Table 4.1 Screening Checklist

Name _____ Date _____

Address _____ Telephone _____

Birthdate _____ Marital Status _____

Education _____

Others in the Household

Names	Age	Sex	Relationship

Health Problems _____

Medications _____

Mental Health Problems:

Panic attacks or phobias _____ Depression _____

Suicide thoughts or attempts _____ Substance abuse _____

Have you had this problem before? _____ What did you do? _____

What helped? _____ What have you tried now? _____

Name of counselor or physician _____

Relationships:

Parents _____ Children _____

Spouse _____ Neighbors _____

Friends _____ Coworkers _____

Employer _____

Finances: Able to pay bills _____ Able to manage funds _____ Adequate income _____

Legal: Any court actions _____

Death: Who died? _____ Relationship _____

Age _____ Date of death _____ Cause _____

Length of illness _____

Circle One

Funeral   Memorial Service   No Observance

Circle One

Burial   Cremation   Ashes: Scattered   Buried   In A Crypt   At Home

History of Significant Deaths:

Person	Date	Cause
Mother		
Father		
Children		
Spouse		
Siblings		
Friends		
Other		

Other Losses: Job _____ Home _____ Financial _____ Pet _____

Other _____

What is bothering you the most at this time? _____

Why do you want to attend a bereavement support group? _____

What do you want to achieve (goals)? _____

first instance the bereaved will appreciate your interest; in the latter they will resent your prying. Use the checklist as a reminder, not as a form that must be completed verbatim.

GOALS

What is to be accomplished in a bereavement support group? Why should anyone attend? What can a bereaved person hope to get out of it?

Bereavement support groups are more than a collection of nice people going through a bad time. There is a purpose. Something is supposed to happen.

Clarity of purpose distinguishes successful groups from unsuccessful ones. If the facilitator and the group members know the purpose of the group, it is easier to focus the discussion. Rambling dialogue that wanders from the theme can be redirected if the group goals are clear. If the goals are stated, the facilitator and the group members can readily avoid tangents by bringing the speaker back to the reason everybody is there.

Group Goals

The overall purpose of bereavement support groups is to provide support to those who have experienced the loss of a loved one—to afford an environment where the bereaved can help each other through their pain and sorrow, to see each other emerge from the experience able to survive and become stronger.

A list of goals might be the following:

The participants will understand the normal grief reaction.
The participants will move through grief at their own pace.
The participants will be able to build satisfying new lives.
The participants will be able to treasure their memories while they build new traditions.
The participants will renew their resources for living.
The participants will acknowledge and understand their losses.
The participants will be able to adjust to lives without their loved ones.
The participants will reinvest themselves in their own lives and find gratifications.
The participants will learn to appreciate the fact that they are alive and can develop in new directions.

Goals will differ from group to group depending on the focus. A beginning bereavement group will concentrate on dealing with the reality of the loss. A transitional group may devote more time to individual growth and problem solving. A graduate group may center around intellectual and social pursuits. Screen the bereaved for appropriate placement in the different types of groups. The newly bereaved will feel out of place in a graduate group. They will not be ready to engage in cheery social occasions. The bereaved who have suffered through their loss and are ready to move on will become impatient with mourners who are intent on coming to grips with their loss. The bereaved will screen themselves if they know what groups are available. They will know whether they want talking support or an opportunity to develop and enrich their life-styles.

Some goals for the transitional and graduate groups will be the same as for the newly bereaved. Some will be altogether different. It is impossible to be all things to all the bereaved. Decide on the focus.

Participant Goals

The bereaved have their own goals. They do not attend support groups because they have nothing else to do. Part of the screening process is determining why the prospective participants want to attend the group and what they hope to get out of it. If their wishes coincide with the group goals, there is a happy meeting of need and service. If the bereaved person's goals are removed from what can be expected from the bereavement group process, the person will have to change the goals or be referred for help from another source. Groups populated by individuals with agendas that do not match the facilitators' plans for the group will fail, and worse, they will fail in frustration and fury. No one will be satisfied (Garvin, 1974).

Goals are important ethically. The facilitators and participants should be working toward the same end. Neither should try to pervert the established and agreed-upon goals because of personal or devious intent. This is not ethical, and it will not work. Similar goals bring trust. Going in different directions brings disappointment.

Goals are also important empirically. If the group leaders and participants have no goals, they do not know when or if they have achieved what they planned.

Goals have to be realistic. Is there time to achieve them? Are the resources for achieving them available? If the goals are realistic and each member's goal is compatible with the others', there is a consensus that leads to positive progress. The more precise the goals, the more likely it is that they will be accomplished.

Many of the bereaved will be unable to state specific goals because of their internal disorganization and their unfamiliarity with what they can expect from a support group. They will, however, be able to state that they want help to feel better, to find out what to do, to meet others who understand, to have a place to go where they are accepted, and to do something for themselves (DiGiulio, 1989). These are all worthwhile and appropriate goals. The bereaved can presume that their hopes about the group will be realized. The facilitators will explain how the group will help, what may make them feel better, how they will learn what works for others, and why those who attend will understand.

Group leaders find that some participants report that they decided to attend the support group because a friend or relative made them or because they hope to find a mate. The first is not a goal, and the latter may not occur. Nevertheless, those reasons do not preclude support group attendance and success. But the bereaved must be told what they can reasonably expect and must be given the opportunity to decide if they still want to participate. The leaders can help them devise personal and possible goals (Palmer & Watt, 1987).

Cross-goals are reflected in evaluations. Statements expressing disappointment and the wish that there had been social activity, or tangible assistance, statements that the group was too depressing, that no one understood, or that spirituality, or some other approach or cure, should have been emphasized, let the facilitators know that the participants were in the wrong group or needed referrals to other resources in addition to the bereavement support group.

Mutual exploration of need and service leads to better feelings all around. The facilitators will sense success, and the participants will acknowledge that they got what they came for.

GUIDELINES

The facilitators set the guidelines for the group. They can be written out and distributed, but they should be set out verbally at the beginning of a closed-end group and whenever new participants join an open-end group. Guidelines or rules are helpful for the facilitators and for the bereaved. They foster the group's functioning because they set parameters and give all those involved something they can count on. The following are some suggested rules:

Confidentiality. Nothing that is brought up in the group should leave the group. Names, situations, and anecdotes should not be shared with anyone who is not part of the group.

Time of meeting. The group will start promptly at the designated time and always end after the agreed amount of time has elapsed.

Number of sessions. The bereaved who attend a closed-end group are asked to commit to the entire series. If something comes up, they are urged to call the facilitator to explain why they cannot come, so that the information can be shared with the group. The attendees are told that once they start working together they become a unit, and everyone in the group develops a concern for all the others in the group. Since there is caring, there is an obligation to report in.

No shoulds, oughts, or musts. Group members can be helpful to each other by listening, showing understanding, and sharing what has made them feel better, but no one knows what another person should do. The group gives support, not advice. Shoulds, oughts, and musts are not helpful and not allowed.

Equal air time. Establish an equal-opportunity-for-verbal-expression rule. State that no one person will be allowed to monopolize the group. When this occurs, the group leader will intervene to make sure that everybody who wants to talk, gets to talk. By the same token, no one is required to talk.

Expression of feelings. All feelings are acceptable, and all group members are urged to express their feelings. The more each member puts into the group, the more that member will get out of the group.

Breaks. Announce whether there will be breaks, when they will occur, and how long they will be, and tell everyone where the bathroom is. Let people know that they may come and go as they need to. They can usually accommodate themselves to the break time if they can count on its happening at the scheduled time.

Telephone numbers and addresses. If telephone numbers and addresses are to be shared with the group, announce that intention, giving everyone the opportunity to decline.

No smoking. Most people would expect that the group hold to a no-smoking rule.

Other. Other rules may also be appropriate, such as a rule that no new members be accepted into a closed-end group after the second session, or a rule that friends and family members are not invited to attend (Rossa, 1993).

Rules can be added, abandoned, or revised. The fewer, the simpler, and the more generally applicable the rules, the more effective they are. Within general guidelines, the facilitator wants the group to be as comfortable and flexible as possible.

Bereavement group facilitators, always looking for ways to be more helpful, will learn as they go along, because each group experience brings new understanding and insight. Of course, the facilitators always hope to be profound, saying just the right thing, at the right time and in the right way. Although the profound statement that is exactly right does occur, more often it is the combination of support, organization, programming, and information that makes the profound impression that helps the bereaved.

When setting up bereavement support groups, nothing can be neglected. It is great to have outstanding facilitators, but if the ambiance of the setting is negative and other details are neglected, crucial elements of the program are missing. The desire to do a good job is not enough. The evidence of doing a good job is what counts. Happily, if the planning and follow-through are achieved in a competent, caring, and considerate manner, the group will be successful. The rewards that come from conducting effective bereavement support groups are well worth the effort.

Chapter 5

Structured Bereavement Support Groups

Structured groups are closed-end groups designed to cover certain topics for a designated population over an established period of time. Unstructured groups are ongoing groups that meet on a regular basis. They may be established to meet the needs of a specified group of mourners or be open to anyone in grief. They may have a regular routine or format, but the bereaved may come and go as they desire. There is no fixed ending date.

ADVANTAGES AND DISADVANTAGES

Structured bereavement groups have many advantages over unstructured bereavement groups and some disadvantages.

The advantages of a structured closed end group are:

1 The participants feel a sense of closure, since the group has a beginning and an ending time.

2 The population can be defined by loss, age, compatibility, length of grief, ability to use the group process, or any other criterion selected.

3 The agenda can be planned to meet the needs of the bereaved who were picked to attend the support group.

4 It is easier to find facilitators to lead groups for a short period of time than to find leaders who will commit to leading a long-term, ongoing group.

5   Facilitators and group members do not burn out or get tired of each other.

6   Space can be found more easily for a limited time than for ongoing meetings.

7   As the bereaved move into different phases of their grief process, they can repeat the series and use the support and information from a slightly altered perspective.

8   The bereaved feel a sense of accomplishment because they have completed the series of meetings.

9   The bereaved and the facilitators do not have the problem of the participants' outgrowing the group and wanting to move on to other activities but not wanting to leave the support group.

Some of the disadvantages of structured bereavement groups are:

1   The bereaved cannot come and go as they please.

2   If the bereaved miss the series, they have to wait until another group of meetings is scheduled.

3   If the support group is designed to meet the needs of a certain population of grievers, others who are also in need cannot attend.

4   If group support is needed for a longer period, it is not available, as the group terminates at the set time.

5   Because the number of meetings is limited, it is not as easy for the group members to bond with each other as when they attend a support group over a longer period of time.

6   Group members who progress at a different pace than the rest of the group do not have time to catch up. They may still be grappling with issues brought up in session one when the group is disbanded.

NUMBER OF SESSIONS

Each series of a structured bereavement support group meet a specific number of times with an established agenda. The group is closed after the optimum number of participants register for the sessions. How many sessions should there be, and how many participants should attend each series?

The number of sessions in a closed-end group varies from six to twelve. There is no particular rationale for the number of meetings in a series, except that five is too few and more than twelve is too many. The sessions take place once a week. This timetable is based more on tradition than on a thought-out plan that weighs the benefits. However, once-a-week sessions are right in that enough happens in a week that the participants have something to talk about; such a timetable also allows them time to take in and integrate what they learned in the previous session. Sessions are held in the morning, the afternoon, or the evening, depending on the group served. Morning and afternoon times are generally offered to older bereaved, and late afternoon and evening times to children and working-age mourners.

The number attending is limited. Eight to ten is about right if it is to be a sharing support group. Space is the only limit if the group is more educational in nature. Sometimes education and sharing are combined, with the speaker making a presentation in the first part of the session and the larger group then breaking into smaller ones for discussion. Each small discussion group has its own facilitator.

The amount of time scheduled for each session varies from one hour to two and one-half hours. The one-hour session generally consists of sharing by the group members. The one-and-one-half-hour session is divided with one hour for talking together and one-half hour for refreshments and socializing. Two-hour sessions allow one and one-half hours for discussion and a half hour for refreshments and socializing, or one hour for a speaker and one hour for small-group discussion. Two-and-one-half-hour group sessions often try to combine all the aspects by allowing time for a presentation, group sharing, and refreshments and socializing.

There is no universally perfect format. What works for one group and one facilitator may not work for others. The facilitators set the time based on their own interests, abilities, and time and the needs of the participants. Trial-and-error is often the basis for the final decision. One group of participants that met for six sessions consistently lobbied for more time together. When the facilitator added a seventh session, only one member of the group showed up. The participants may be reluctant to leave the group, but still know when they have obtained what they needed from the group. They may have other projects that take their time or have some internal clock that tells them when it is time to move on. On the other hand, it is not as though there is not enough material for more than six sessions. The topics are limited only by the interest of the participants and the imagination of the facilitator. One rule of thumb is that the more educational material that is presented and the more people that attend, the more sessions there should be.

When deciding on the number of sessions, other considerations may come into play. Prospective group members may drop out to go on vacations, entertain relatives around the holidays, or get out of the habit of attending if a session is cancelled because of a holiday or because the facilitator has a conflict. Try to pick a time for the series that will allow for the fewest scheduling problems. There is no way to set the time to meet the needs of everyone, but the facilitator will soon discover that some times of the year are busier than others.

One time a week is the conventionally accepted schedule for the meetings, and it is probably the optimum schedule as well. People are busy. There are other obligations. They can plan to go to sessions over a period of time on a designated day of the week. A week gives the participants time to think about what they have learned and to have experiences that they may want to share with the group. A weekly meeting does not infringe on the normal schedules of the bereaved, allowing them to maintain what is intact. Meetings more than one time a week may take them from their friends and relatives or other obligations and activities and have them invest too much time and energy into the bereavement support group. This subtracts from their usual life-styles and gives the support group too much importance in their lives. The bereaved should be able to rely on the support from the group, but the support group should not take over their lives by drawing them away from day-to-day exertions, concerns, and satisfactions. Bereavement support provides assistance with living, not a reason for living. The group may be a welcome retreat but should not become the crucial part of their ongoing life.

If a closed-end bereavement group is heavily advertised and the response is good-to-overwhelming, back-up plans must be made to accommodate all those who are interested and appropriate group candidates. The time for the bereaved to attend a support group is when they feel they are ready. If the group is to be held for ten participants, and twenty-five sign up, an additional, concurrent group can be held, another group can be scheduled that will follow on the heels of the first group, or the entire number can meet together with an adjusted format that includes educational presentations followed by small-group discussions.

Eight to ten participants are the optimum number for a sharing support group (Nudel, 1987). This number allows for individual participation, accommodates diverse ideas and suggestions, and minimizes pressure on those who do not want to speak up. It is a large enough number that there continues to be a group when some of the participants drop out or miss sessions. Fifteen regular attendees is the top limit. Any number larger than that is no longer a support group. It is a crowd or an audience. Educational and social groups can accommodate any number. Discussion-type support groups need smaller numbers to be effective. The bereaved have enough frustrations in their lives without having to feel thwarted in their bereavement support group. If there are too many people, the more retiring will feel as though they do not get to talk about their problems or that no one in the group is interested in hearing from them.

People's lives are programmed for one-hour intervals of time. If the bereavement support group is scheduled for longer than one hour, a break will have to be a routine part of the meeting. The format can be stretched to one and one-half hours, but do not try to go beyond that amount of time. People get restless, their minds wander, physical needs become pressing and they start thinking about their other responsibilities. They are getting together for relief from pain and do not want to be in a situation that causes them anxiety or agitation.

There will be people in any group who want more time and will be unable to quit at the end of an hour or an hour and one-half. If that is the case, the facilitator can plan to talk with them briefly at the end of each session to help them ease out of the group, giving them additional time to appease their need to express themselves further. There will be people in the group who need more than they can get in a support group. The facilitator can arrange to see them individually or refer them to an appropriate resource.

All of the foregoing recommendations are based on what works for many of the facilitators of bereavement support groups. A new facilitator starting a support group will do well to heed them and not make the mistakes others have made trying to find the right formula. Nevertheless there are exceptions. Some facilitators, in some areas, with some bereaved have altogether unique situations and unique formats. Just because something does not work for one person does not mean that it will not work for another.

TOPICS FOR STRUCTURED SESSIONS

It is more comfortable for the facilitator and for the bereaved attending the support group if there is an agenda. That makes them feel more secure. They want guidance and want to feel as though they are being cared for. They want to think of their leader as knowledgeable and in charge.

The facilitator can take charge in the first meeting by pointing out the responsibilities of those who attend the group, letting them know the structure of the group, and laying out the plans for the first and the ensuing sessions. The members then know what will be asked of them and what to expect, and they can be reassured that they do not have to say or do anything that they do not want to say or do.

The rest of this chapter will outline possible plans for a structured bereavement support group for those who have suffered the death of a spouse. This design adapts to support groups for other types of loss as well.

SESSION ONE-LEARNING ABOUT GRIEF

Topics

1   Group structure and expectations.
2   What each participant wants from the group.
3   Personal experience with grief.
4   What has happened up to now.
5   Getting acquainted.

Objectives

1   Participants will be able to speak about their grief.
2   Participants will identify what they want from the support group.
3   Participants will develop a beginning trust in the group members and the group process.
4   Participants will make a commitment to work on their grief.

Materials Needed

1   Name tags.
2   Sign-in sheet.
3   Slips for names and telephone numbers.
4   A basket to hold the name and telephone number slips.
5   Paper and pencils for written exercise.
6   Handouts (see page 88).
7   Table to sit around and chairs.
8   Refreshments.
9   Tissues.
10 Chalk or enamel board or flip chart.

Activities

1   Group structure and expectations.
    a. Introduce yourselves.
    b. Give housekeeping information, such as where the bathrooms are, how long the session will last, when the break occurs, the schedule, and the topics for the rest of the sessions.
    c. State the rules (Worden, 1988):

    • Confidentiality
    • Equal air time
    • No shoulds, oughts, or musts
    • If you cannot attend, please call.
    • Feelings are accepted and encouraged.

- No one has to speak if they do not want to.
- The group will start and end on time.

d. Introduce the topic for session one. Explain that this is the getting acquainted session and that we start by talking about why we are here and telling about our own losses. If someone does not want to speak, he or she can say "Pass," and no questions will be asked.

Warn everyone that this is the most difficult and most emotional of all the sessions. They should not let the distress of the first session keep them from attending the rest of the sessions. If they continue to come, they will start feeling better and may even have fun. If someone in the session has attended the series previously, ask that person to verify these statements.

2   Find out what the participants are expecting from the group: Go around the room asking people to introduce themselves, giving their names, any other identifying information that seems pertinent, and saying why they have come to the group and what they hope to get out of it. Accept and reinforce all the answers. You may want to ask for a volunteer to start the discussion or select one person who appears ready to speak.

3   Sharing the personal grief story: The facilitator can have the participants tell the entire group of their loss, or pair up the group members and have them exchange the stories between the two of them. For a larger group, the twosome interchange is effective because too many grief stories take too much group time and become emotionally exhausting for the group.

The use of the dyad is also effective in a smaller group. The bereaved can be paired off and take five to ten minutes to tell each other the story of their loss. Then have every person introduce the one they talked to, telling something about the individual and explaining the circumstances of the death.

However the facilitator decides to handle the sharing of the grief experience, the process for telling should be made clear. The facilitator can explain what information is requested, how much time is allotted, and, if possible, write the instructions on a chalk or enamel board or flip chart. The instructions might be as follows:

Take two minutes to tell

- when your loved one died.
- the cause of death.
- some of your feelings.

Two minutes may not seem long, and it is not. However, if ten participants take two minutes each, the time used is twenty minutes. This is a large segment of a one- or one and one-half-hour session. Some people will take slightly more time, and some will take a little less. If the facilitator has suffered a loss similar to that of the group members, or can talk about another's loss, it is good to give an example, using this story, of what should be included in the two-minute presentation (Farra, 1986).

As the group members express their feelings, the facilitator may want to take notes on all of the feelings mentioned and/or write them on the chalk or enamel board or flip chart.

After the feelings are posted, the group can be told that all these and other feelings are normal and are part of the normal grief process. There may be other feelings that they will want to add to the list. They may also want to add behaviors, physical reactions, and descriptions of how their social lives changed. The list may look like this:

Emotional	Physical	Social	Behavioral
Sad	Fatigue	Fifth wheel	Withdrawn
Angry	Flare-ups of	Said no to	Kept busy
Anxious	chronic	invitations	Stayed in bed
Guilty	conditions	Self-conscious	New skills
Lonely	Crying	Loss of	Lost life-style
Resentful	Empty feeling	companionship	Have to care
Denial	Sleeping	Avoid places	for self
Fear	problems	Make new	Restless
Flash-backs	Eating	friends	
Relief	problems		

4   What has happened up to now?

Distribute round, white, paper plates, or have the participants draw a large circle on a piece of paper. Draw a circle on the chalk or enamel board or flip chart. Ask the group members to divide their pie to show where their energy is presently going. What amount goes toward self-care, friendships, household duties, work, or maintenance activities? Draw your own pie chart on the display board. This is an example of what the group members are to do to depict how their time is being spent. When they have completed the task, ask them to draw another pie that will show how they spent their time before their loved one died. Then instruct them to draw a third pie graph that will display how they want to spend their time six months from now.

This exercise helps the bereaved see how their lives have changed and lets them know how their lives can change. It indicates the stress of change they are experiencing and implies that there is hope for a future of their choice. If there are some who cannot imagine what they would like to have in the future or cannot bring themselves to draw it, let them know that that is all right. Have some of the participants discuss their drawings. This might nudge those who could not come up with any sort of picture of their future.

5   Getting acquainted: Explain that a basket will be passed containing the participants' names and numbers written on slips of paper. Each group member is to draw one and call that person sometime during the week. Also, unless individual group members direct otherwise, there will be a list of the names, addresses, and telephone numbers of all the participants, so each person present can call anyone they want to.

6   Homework: Participants are urged to keep journals, which they may share with the group. There is no requirement that they do so. Keeping a journal gives them an outlet for their feelings, helps them focus their

thoughts, and serves as a source of hope. If they look back in a few weeks' time on what they have written, they will see how they have progressed.

7   Announcements: Save the announcements for last. One announcement that the facilitator will want to make after the first meeting is that the participants can expect dreams. They are not to be alarmed by this. Anytime we focus on a particular topic during the day, that subject will come up in our dreams. They may even appreciate having their loved ones appear in their dreams.

8   One last thought:

You do not live all your minutes at once. You just live the one you are in. You can make it through one minute. You do not have to be strong for that, just one minute. One minute at a time. *(Author unknown)*

A note on seating: The leader may want to note where each participant sits. They have their reasons for picking their particular seating and will more than likely return to that place every session thereafter. Allow this. Some group leaders feel that the members should be required to sit next to different people during each ensuing session, so they can meet and mix. This is not a good idea. It is hard enough to enter a room filled with strangers, with the plan to talk about innermost thoughts and feelings, without having continually to make new decisions about where to sit and to reorient with each session. It is comfortable for the participants to have their own places. That provides a modicum of security. It is fine for them to sit among friends if they came with a group. The only time it would be necessary to break up an established seating order is if a certain set of participants spend so much time talking among themselves that they distract the rest of the group members.

Because this group session addresses a general view of grief and the sharing of feelings, the format and topics are appropriate for any loss that involves someone who was part of the everyday lives of the bereaved. The major differences among the participants will be in the social and behavioral reactions listed under item 3, after the telling of the personal grief story. If the loved ones who died were not integral to the life-styles of the bereaved, the pie chart exercise will not be meaningful to them.

Table 5.1   Handout for Session One

Symptoms of Grief

Physical

1. Hyperactive or underactive
2. Feelings of unreality
3. Physical distress such as chest pains, abdominal pains, headaches, nausea
4. Change in appetite
5. Weight change
6. Fatigue
7. Sleeping problems
8. Restlessness
9. Crying and sighing
10. Feelings of emptiness
11. Shortness of breath
12. Tightness in the throat

Emotional

1. Numbness
2. Sadness
3. Anger
4. Fear
5. Relief
6. Irritability
7. Guilt
8. Loneliness
9. Longing
10. Anxiety
11. Meaninglessness
12. Apathy
13. Vulnerability
14. Abandonment

Social

1. Overly sensitive
2. Dependent
3. Withdrawn
4. Avoid others
5. Lack of initiative
6. Lack of interest

Behavioral

1. Forgetfulness
2. Searching for the deceased
3. Slowed thinking
4. Dreams of the deceased
5. Sense the loved one's presence
6. Wandering aimlessly
7. Trying not to talk about loss in order to help others feel comfortable around them
8. Needing to retell the story of the loved one's death

Help Through Grief

1. Be patient with yourself. Do not compare yourself to others. Go through mourning at your own pace.
2. Admit you are hurting and go with the pain.
3. Apply cold or heat to your body, whichever feels best.
4. Ask for and accept help.
5. Talk to others.
6. Face the loss.
7. Stop asking "Why?" and ask "What will I do now?"
8. Recognize that a bad day does not mean that all is lost.
9. Rest.
10. Exercise.
11. Keep to a routine.
12. Introduce pleasant changes into your life.
13. Know that you will survive.
14. Take care of something alive, such as a plant or a pet.
15. Schedule activities to help yourself get through weekends and holidays.
16. Find someone who needs your help.
17. Accept your feelings as part of the normal grief reaction.
18. Postpone major decisions whenever possible.
19. Do something you enjoy doing.
20. Write in a journal.
21. Be around people.
22. Schedule time alone.
23. Do not overdo.
24. Eat regularly.

SESSION TWO-REACTIONS TO GRIEF

Topics

1 The grief process.
2 Reactions to the grief process.
3 What are you doing now that you did not know you could do, or did not do before?

Objectives

1 Participants will understand the grief process.
2 Participants will identify where they are in the grief process.
3 Participants will recognize what they are able to do.

Materials Needed

1 Name tags.
2 Sign-in sheet.
3 Slips for names and telephone numbers.
4 A basket to hold the name and telephone slips.
5 Paper and pencils for written exercise.
6 Handouts (see pages 93-94).
7 Table to sit around and chairs.
8 Refreshments.
9 Tissues.
10 Chalk or enamel board or flip chart.

Activities

1 Have the name tags ready for the participants. This will help them feel welcomed and expected.
2 Welcome everyone. If someone is not present, announce why not. Plan to follow up on anyone who has not returned to the group or called. Accept dropouts but find out the reason.
3 Ask whether anyone has anything left over from the week before that they want to bring up or ask about, or whether anyone has something that he or she needs to discuss. If someone raises a burning issue, ask for help from the members of the support group. They will make suggestions based on their own experiences. The facilitator may keep the discussion going or bring it to a close, depending on the process. If no one puts forward an issue to talk about, the facilitator may move on to the planned topic.
4 Describe the grief process. The grief process starts with learning of the loved one's death, progresses to realizing that the loved one will

never again be a tangible part of one's life, and changes to learning to live life without the loved one's presence. These phases go by various names (see chapter 1, phases of grief). Widowed Persons Service calls them *impact, recoil,* and *accommodation.* Impact is felt when the knowledge of the death arrives. Recoil is the time when the feelings from the shock start coming back. Accommodation occurs when the mourner realizes that life will go on. All of this is normal grief. It is important that all participants recognize that what they are going through has a beginning, that there is relief, and that the process is a normal part of healing. They are not going crazy or being bizarre. They are experiencing a normal grief reaction. They will survive, and they will survive gloriously.

Write Impact, Recoil, and Accommodation on the chalk or enamel board or flip chart. Ask the group to help you fill in columns under each word.

Ask them how they felt when they learned their loved one had died. Write down the feelings under Impact. Ask how long the feelings lasted. Some might say that they are still feeling shock, or that the feelings come and go. Others may say that the feelings lasted one day, or for a few hours. There is no correct answer. However anyone feels is the right way for him or her.

Ask how the participants felt when the feelings surged back, when the numbness wore off, and they realized that dead was dead. When did this happen? At the funeral? Before the funeral? After the funeral? When the relatives all went home? Has it happened yet? Some may say that they still think they see their loved one and still search for him or her. This is normal. Grief does not travel in a straight line. Ask how long this phase lasts. Inasmuch as there is no concrete answer, anything the support group members suggest is acceptable.

Ask if anyone has reached accommodation, when they know that they are going to make it. Ask the group members for those feelings. What are they, or what do they imagine they might be (Farra, 1986)?

If the participants do not come up with many answers, the leader can use some of the feelings that were mentioned in the last session when the participants shared the stories of their grief. The list might look something like this:

Impact	Recoil	Accommodation
Denial	Anger	There's more
Numb	Fear	Look ahead
Relief	Panic	It is up to me
Can't remember	Disoriented	It's O.K.
Empty	Sick	I'll make it
Shock	Exhausted	Healthy again

If the group is made up of the newly bereaved, they may not be able to identify with the concept of accommodation. They can be offered hope that this stage will be reached. It will take time and work, but it is within their grasp.

Along with discussion of the grief reaction and the understanding that the progress through mourning is a series of ups and downs must come the reassurance that a down day, or an uncontrolled bereavement reaction, does not mean that all is lost. It only means that something has reminded the bereaved person of the lost loved one and that an overwhelming emotion, which is part of the normal grief process, is being experienced. It is not a permanent setback. Ask the group what triggers these responses. Is it music, smells, places, people, food? Go around the room and ask each person to identify the poignant memory that does it for them. Is it what people say, going to the store, a certain room? Knowing will help the participants cope with their feelings.

As the support group members relate their most difficult times and troubling memories, they will recognize that they are going through a normal process (Rubin & Rubin, 1992). They will help each other understand that this is all part of the healing feelings of grieving. They will also be helped by the support they get from one another. They will ask what others did in similar situations, or they will talk about what helped them get through bad times. If this support does not evolve spontaneously, the group leader can prompt it by asking if any of the participants have experiences to share. The process relies on mutual support. The sooner they start supporting one another, the more effective the process.

4a Optional exercise: Refer to the handout depicting the circle of grief (Spangler, 1988) and the zigzag of emotional ups and downs (Figure 5.1). If there is time, have the participants identify where they are in the circle of grief. Also ask them to write out what causes their emotional storms. These events or memories can be entered on the low points of the zigzag line. These exercises will illustrate for the bereaved the fact that they are generally going forward, and a setback is not permanent.

Some of the group members will talk about the sadness that is evoked when they are around friends or relatives. If this topic is brought up, now may be the right time to talk about changed relationships with friends and relatives, instead of waiting for the time when it is on the agenda. No planned subject in any support group is ever written in concrete. Each facilitator needs to be flexible enough to go along with what seems to be of consequence at the moment. Some of the most productive sessions respond to the needs of the moment.

5 What are you doing now that you did not know you could do or did not do before? This topic will be met with groans because everyone will be doing things they did not do before and performing tasks they never wanted to do. Some of what they now have to do brings anger and anguish. Nevertheless, the focus is on strength, ability, and self-confidence. Each person who accomplishes something they never thought they could or would do should be complimented, encouraged, and praised.

Group members will criticize themselves because they divided responsibilities between themselves and their loved ones, or they never learned to do certain things, or they did most things with their loved ones. Acknowledge these feelings, but explain that if they had not done it the way they did, they would not have the fond memories they now have. No one can live life in a way that totally accommodates an inevitable death. Besides, when people live together it is efficient and makes sense to divide duties. It does not pay for everyone to do everything. Because there is a division of duties, however, the parts of ourselves that we do not use atrophy, as a muscle would. If we do not use an arm, that arm weakens. When we never take care of the car or cook a meal, those skills atrophy. But strength can be regained. Skills can be learned or relearned.

6   Telephone buddies: Have each participant draw the name and telephone number of their telephone buddy for the week.

7   Homework: Ask the group members to continue to write in their journals and to chart their ups and downs.

8   Announcements: Remind the support group participants of the dates of the rest of the sessions and tell them again of the general topics to be discussed.

9   One last thought:

When we cannot bear to be alone, it means we do not properly value the only companion we will have from birth to death—ourselves. *(Eda LaShan in Long Island, N.Y., Newsday)*

A note to the facilitator: Although the group leader should report on each member who has missed the group, do not talk about any members without their permission, and do not make critical comments about those who may have dropped out or complained that the group made them feel worse.

To adapt this session to a parent group, leave out the section on what participants are doing that they did not do before and substitute a question on how the loss has affected them since they no longer have certain responsibilities and obligations. If the bereaved did not live with the deceased, but were involved in their lives, ask them about their changed attitudes in regard to the activities that they and the deceased previously enjoyed together.

The facilitators will want to revise the Table 5.2 handout, deleting items 2, 13, and 14 if the group is not for the widowed. Items 6, 8, and 14 may also be omitted if the deceased is a child, sibling, or parent.

Figure 5.1 Handout for Session Two

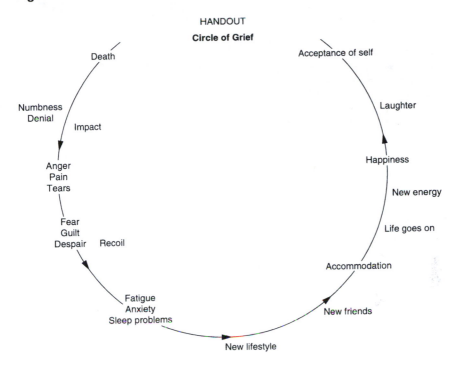

HANDOUT

Circle of Grief

Death

Numbness
Denial

Impact

Anger
Pain
Tears

Fear
Guilt
Despair   Recoil

Fatigue
Anxiety
Sleep problems

New lifestyle

Acceptance of self

Laughter

Happiness

New energy

Life goes on

Accommodation

New friends

Ups and Downs of Grief

Table 5.2   Second Handout for Session Two

Some of the facts of life after a death are the following:

1. People want you to be "fine," not unhappy.
2. It is a couple society.
3. You may feel that you are going crazy.
4. Tears come unbidden.
5. Physicians want to give you medication.
6. Finances change, frequently for the worse.
7. Some friends and acquaintances drift away.
8. Skills that have not been used have atrophied and need to be relearned.
9. There is anger, and guilt about the anger.
10. You may question your faith.
11. People do not know what to say to you.
12. People will try to comfort you by saying, "It is for the best."
13. Widowers may remarry soon. Widows probably won't.
14. Sex is a problem.
15. You feel vulnerable to exploitation.
16. You feel incomplete. Something is missing.
17. There are Whys and If Onlys.
18. People may avoid talking about the deceased, thinking that they do not want to upset you.
19. Chronic health problems flare up.
20. People will want to give you advice or tell you what to do.
21. Relationships change.

SESSION THREE-GRIEF AND STRESS

Topics

1 The need for grief.
2 Coping with holidays and anniversaries.
3 Stress and self-care.

Objectives

1 The participants will recognize the healing power of grief.
2 The participants will learn some coping skills for dealing with holidays and anniversaries.
3 The participants will look at their individual stress and find ways to take care of themselves.

Materials Needed

1 Name tags.
2 Sign-in sheet.
3 Slips for names and telephone numbers.
4 A basket to hold the name and telephone slips.
5 Handouts (see pages 98-99).
6 Table to sit around and chairs.
7 Refreshments.
8 Tissues.
9 Chalk or enamel board or flip chart.

Activities

1 Welcome everyone. Follow up with information on anyone who missed the previous group if they have given permission to share information.
2 Ask whether anyone has a pressing issue or a comment to share before the group gets started on the planned topics.
3 The need for grief: Everybody in the support group is there because of the pain. They want to be rid of it. It is helpful for the group members to understand that grief is more than just misery. It is a healing process. It can be characterized as an open wound that requires time and care so that proper healing can take place. Part of the support group's purpose is to make it possible for those in grief to come together so that they can help one another heal well.

The pain of grief is a process. Even though it seems to continue without ceasing, there is change. Although it may feel as though the grief is intensifying, it is not better or worse; it is change, and it is healing. As each individual is unique, so is each grief. There are similarities in grief, as there are likenesses among human beings, but no one can predict accurately another person's grief process.

What changes have the bereavement group members noticed in their grief process? The emphasis on change is an emphasis on healing. It delivers the bereaved from the judgment of whether they are doing better or worse.

4   Coping with the holidays and anniversaries: The Thanksgiving, Christmas, Hanukkah, and New Year's holidays put a damper on the entire last two months of the year for many of the bereaved (Wolfelt, 1993). These are difficult holidays for those in grief. Any support group series that falls around that time of the year needs to address the stress that occurs with nationally advertised and observed holidays. However, coping with holidays can be discussed in any of the group sessions, as some special day is always coming up. Easter, Valentine's Day, Mother's or Father's Day, Memorial Day, Labor Day, or Independence Day—all are likely to hold some special significance and memories for the survivor. The facilitators will want to ask what the group members did in the past, what they did for the last holiday, what holidays they have experienced since the death of the loved one, how they plan to manage, what suggestions they have received (although advice is not allowed in bereavement support groups, there is no way to prevent relatives, friends, and neighbors from giving lots of it), and how people they know handled the holidays after they were bereaved. The facilitator can share information on how other bereaved people coped with certain traditional holidays. If there are few ideas, it may be because the bereaved have not yet faced this problem. There may also be no suggestions because they have not given it any thought or are overwhelmed by the idea. Discussion of some of the proposals in the "Help for the Holidays" handout (see Table 5.3) may be worthwhile.

Anniversaries of marriages, the death, and other significant events, such as birthdays, are never forgotten. They may slip the conscious mind, but the subconscious never forgets. The bereaved will be reminded by physical and emotional reactions. These are days that need to be acknowledged and observed. An individual's life bears remembering; it must count for something. This is crucial for the surviving children and for adults too. One way to do this is to remember the loved ones on important anniversaries. The group members need the opportunity to explore their fears and their pain and talk about their plans.

5   Stress and self-care: Any life-style change causes stress. A loss affects everybody's life. The death of a loved one is a major loss and a traumatic stressor for the survivor. Many of the symptoms of grief are symptoms of stress. Fatigue that is not relieved by rest, impaired ability to concentrate, denial, difficulty making decisions, irritability, forgetfulness, susceptibility to physical illness because of lowered resistance, feelings of unreality, the need to cry, hypersensitivity, a negative outlook, and a sense of vulnerability are a few of the signs of both stress and grief. Grief is synonymous with stress.

Because everybody has had losses in their lives, and all have experienced stress, this comparison gives the bereaved a sense of control and relief. Ask them to look at losses and other stresses, to recall their reactions, and to think about what helped them. How they handled stress in the past is a good indicator of how they will handle their present stress from a primary loss. The leader will want to concentrate on the stress relievers that worked. Many coping techniques are not necessarily helpful, and some can be dangerous. Self-care during stress means that the bereaved will care enough about themselves to make sure that they take healthy initiatives, even though they may not feel like it.

The facilitator will want to concentrate on good health habits, techniques to enhance self-esteem, ways to develop and maintain support, methods for finding pleasurable pursuits, and some ways to find quick relief. My book *Quick Fixes: 303 Ways to Help Yourself Before the Therapist Arrives* is recommended to the facilitator. Excerpts from it can be used as handouts and for discussion.

If one of the group members knows relaxation techniques, he or she may be willing to teach the skill to the rest of the group, if time allows. Do not, however, let the support group become a stress reduction/relaxation group. The topic continues to be grief. It is better to set another time to teach relaxation, outside of the support group, or refer the participants to other resources in the community where this technique is taught.

6   Telephone buddies: Each participant will draw a name and telephone number for this week's telephone buddy.

7   Homework: Ask the group if they are writing in their journals. Encourage them to continue. Because relationships with friends and relatives will be discussed in the next session, instruct the group members to write letters to significant friends and relatives in which they say all the things they really want to say. They do not have to mail these letters, and they are not required to share them with the group. They may do so if they want.

8   Announcements: Remind the participants of the upcoming sessions and topics.

9   One last thought:

Life is 10% what we make it and 90% how we take it.

A note to the facilitator: Although the facilitator may not want to take group time to discuss telephone buddies and keeping a journal, it is a good idea to check informally to let the group members know of the facilitator's interest, to determine the amount of follow-through, and to find out how effective these approaches are for the participants.

Using chance to select telephone buddies, providing a different person to call each week, works well because people who do not make the call, or who end up talking to someone they do not like, get a change the next week. They do not feel that they are stuck with unresponsive or incompatible people. On occasion, however, telephone buddies have been assigned on the basis of their loss: The idea is that this will be mutually helpful because people who have lost their loved ones through suicide, sudden death, or a particular disease will have similarities, and a feeling of kinship will develop. People are always fascinated with their own experiences.

Please note how the topics, format, and focus on each group session assists with the grief process, gives hope, and teaches coping skills. The combination is essential to any bereavement program.

The topics and approaches in this session are appropriate and helpful for any bereaved person or groups of people.

Table 5.3   Handout for Session Three

Help for the Holidays

1. Get your fears about the holidays out of your system. Write them down. Know what they are.
2. Plan ahead. Know what you want to do, are willing to do, or do not want to do.
3. See the holidays as a series of small events instead of an endless stream of pain. You can handle one event at a time.
4. Decide if you want to continue with family traditions, alter them, or start all over with your own traditions.
5. Try to keep holiday planning and celebrations simple. Do not ask too much of yourself. Do not get too tired.
6. Put some effort into seeing that someone else has a wonderful holiday. Visit nursing homes. Work on a holiday dinner at a charitable organization. Find satisfaction in doing for others.
7. Go on a trip.
8. Take a friend or relative to a spectator event, such as a play, concert, or sporting event.
9. Talk about your feelings .Cry, laugh. Do not try to hide your honest emotions.
10. Remember your responsibility to yourself. Take care of yourself!
11. Shop early or by mail order if you want to avoid the holiday hoopla.
12. Give yourself a nice present.
13. Decide how you will answer all the cheerful greetings of the holiday season. When you hear "Happy holidays!" you may want to say, "Thanks," "Happy holidays to you," or "I'm trying."
14. Talk about the deceased if you want to. Look for positive memories.

Table 5.4 Second Handout for Session Three

Stress Survival

1. Exercise. Physical exercise changes the body chemistry. Endorphins are manufactured. Endorphins make you feel better.
2. Do something you enjoy that requires your concentration. This will distract you from your present stresses.
3. Do something for someone else. This will increase your self-esteem and give you a feeling of satisfaction.
4. Start and finish a short-term project. This will give you a sense of completion and accomplishment.
5. Sign up for lessons to learn something new. This will aid you in self-discovery, expand your thinking, and bring a new interest into your life.
6. Do something nice for yourself. See yourself as a person who deserves good things in life.
7. Keep up old relationships and try to make new ones. You need a support system.
8. Say yes. Say yes to invitations. Do not cut yourself off from experiences and opportunities.
9. Say no. You do not have to do anything that does not seem right to you.

SESSION FOUR-GRIEF AND RELATIONSHIPS

Topics

1 Changing relationships with friends and relatives.
2 Present roles.
3 Memorabilia.

Objectives

1 The participants will be better able to understand and define relationships with friends and families.
2 The participants will be able to identify their ongoing roles.
3 The participants will be able to examine their memories of the deceased.

Materials Needed

1 Name tags.
2 Sign-in sheet.
3 Slips for the telephone buddy names and numbers.
4 A basket for the telephone buddy slips.
5 Paper, paste, scissors, and magazines for the optional exercise.
6 Handouts (see page 103).
7 Table and chairs.
8 Refreshments.
9 Tissues.
10 Chalk or enamel board or flip chart.

Activities

1 Greet the participants with their prepared name tags.
2 Welcome everyone and report on any group members who could not attend. If someone is not returning to the group, let the rest of the group members know, giving the reason if the participant has agreed that you may do so.
3 Changing relationships with friends and families.

It does not take much to get this topic going. The bereaved will report disappointments, surprises, anger, satisfaction, pleasure, puzzlement, and hurt. Encourage them to look at all of their relationships, including those with siblings, children, parents, in-laws, church and club acquaintances, neighbors, couples, and other friends (AARP, 1988). Listen to the anecdotes. As usual, find out how others in the group have experienced and handled similar circumstances. Help them deal with reality instead of trying to change the way that people act toward them. What can they do to cope with the changed behavior of others?

4 Present roles.

Because roles have changed and treatment by others puts the bereaved in a position of defining relationships and roles, this is a good time to look at which of their roles have continued and which have changed.

An unstructured, but guided, discussion works well. The facilitator can begin by asking the group to call out all their past roles. These can be listed on a chalk or enamel board or a flip chart. The roles are innumerable. Besides relationship roles—parent, sibling, child, spouse—there are job roles; roles as provider, home manager, gardener, and social director. There are community roles as volunteer, consumer, patient, and friend, and special interest roles, as sports fan, craftsperson, biker, collector. Then ask the group which past roles continue into the present. Which past roles have they abandoned that they would like to pick up? What are some of their new roles? This leads to a discussion of their comfort in their new roles and what they can do to help themselves, or to receive help, to function well in their new roles. The leader may want to compile a list of helpful hints to hand out to the participants at the next session.

If there is time and interest, the facilitator can direct the group members in the making of a shared collage or individual ones that illustrates their present roles. They can cut pictures from the magazines and paste or tape them to a sheet of paper. If personal collages are made, each participant can take the finished work home as a reminder of his or her new life. They can also add to the collage as they add new roles.

5 Memorabilia.

The discussion of roles ties into the topic of memorabilia. What knowledge do the participants have from their past (before the traumatic death) that helps them in the present? This information and knowledge is part of their arsenal of important memories. In the same way that they lost some past roles, they may find that some past ways of functioning are no longer effective. The behaviors have had to be discarded, just as they have had to let go of some of their loved one's possessions.

Lead the group discussion to tangible memorabilia. What have they kept? What have they thrown away or given away? Some of the group will advocate getting rid of everything right away. Others will have made no attempt to go through their loved one's belongings. There is no right way. There are individual ways. Accept whatever anybody has done and their reasons for doing so. The participants will make their own decisions on what to save and what to discard, based on their own frames of reference and need.

To further the memorabilia topic, ask the participants to bring mementos or pictures to the next session (Whipple, 1992). The items should recall happy moments, highlights of the relationship, what the bereaved most want to remember, or something that makes them proud. Given these options, even the survivors of unhappy relationships can find something positive that they can share with their fellow mourners.

6   Telephone buddies.

Let the participants draw the name of their telephone buddy for the week.

7   Homework.

Encourage continued writing in their journals. Remind the group members to bring in their memorabilia next week.

8   Announcements.

Announce the number, dates, and topics of upcoming sessions.

9   One last thought:

> After becoming a widow, Dr. Joyce Brothers said in a speech in Prairie Village, Kansas, "You need to be good to yourself. It's not a tribute to the person you have lost to make your life smaller or to not have joy in your life."

A note to the facilitator: With each session there is less need for planned topics. Although a facilitator is needed, the facilitator becomes less important as a source of discussion material and more significant as an air traffic manager who keeps the discussion on track.

As the participants understand the focus of the group and get to know each other better, they will come prepared with their own topics. They will ask for and give help to one another. The facilitator will be pleased to see the group become more and more self-directed.

Working with memories and mementos is appropriate and helpful for any age group and for any bereaved person.

The handout on making friends (Table 5.5) may not be applicable to the problems of some of the bereaved, but it is not inappropriate for anyone. Even bereaved parents may feel the need to make new friends because they may be uncomfortable with the parents of their child's friends or may find that people drift away from them because they are uncomfortable with the family's loss.

Table 5.5   Handout for Session Four

Making New Friends

How to Find Friends

1. Let go of your past and look toward your future.
2. See that you have much of value to give to a friendship.
3. What do you want in a friendship? Someone like you or someone who has different ideas and interests? Someone you can see daily or someone to go out with on occasion?
4. Decide to take the initiative to find friends.
5. Recognize that other people want friends too.

Where to Find Friends

1. Go to places that interest you.
2. Join a health club.
3. Find someone to teach you a new skill.
4. Join an organization.
5. Give a party.
6. Take an adult education course.
7. Go to group therapy.
8. Volunteer.
9. Speak to people in waiting rooms and checkout lines.
10. Join a church group.
11. Take your dog to obedience training.
12. Borrow something and return it with a small token of gratitude.
13. Buy two tickets to an event and invite someone to attend with you.
14. Plant a garden and give vegetables and flowers away.
15. Get the people you know to introduce you to people they know.

How to Make Friends

1. Tune in to the needs and feelings of others.
2. Be accepting of others.
3. Identify interesting events so that you can retell short anecdotes.
4. Engage in small talk about the weather, current events, the parking problem.
5. Ask for advice or an opinion.
6. Give sincere compliments.
7. Be prepared by having something to talk about.
8. Ask for help.
9. Offer help.
10. Ask people questions that will stimulate them to talk about themselves. Where are you from? What do you like about this place?
11. Be open and share something about yourself. But do not pour out your troubles or reveal intimate information.
12. Be an active listener. Learn the sounds and signs of interest—Um-hum, Oh, I see, Wow!—smiles, nods, leaning forward.
13. Tell an amusing story about yourself.
14. Make eye contact.
15. Avoid arguments.
16. Be pleasant and look receptive.
17. Remember names.
18. Don't criticize.
19. Be cheerful.
20. Be compassionate.
21. Let people you like know it.
22. Accept invitations.

SESSION FIVE-GRIEF AND GUILT

Topics

1   Sharing memories.
2   Guilt.

Objectives

1   The participants will learn techniques for retrieving positive memories.
2   The participants will understand their guilt reactions and learn how to deal with them.

Materials Needed

1   Prepared name tags.
2   Sign-in sheet.
3   Slips for the telephone buddy names and numbers.
4   A basket to hold the telephone buddy slips.
5   Handouts (see pages 107-108).
6   Table and chairs.
7   Refreshments.
8   Tissues.
9   Writing material for the group exercise.
10   Chalk or enamel board or flip chart.

Activities

1   Welcome the group members. Report on absences.
Ask for updates, questions, or concerns. Address any that need immediate attention.
2   Sharing memories.
Go around the room and ask each participant, one by one, to share their pictures or mementos. Give everyone time to make their presentation and pass around their items. After everybody has seen one person's contribution, move on to the next one. Make positive comments and express thanks after each individual completes the sharing.
The purpose of the exercise is to honor the loved ones, to help the survivors deal with the reality of the death, to give the bereaved an opportunity to talk about their loved ones, and to help the mourner focus on good, pleasant, proud, and positive memories. The facilitator wants to help the bereaved move from painful memories to poignant memories. This takes time, but it takes work too. If they keep emphasizing the bad times and the unhappy memories and cannot get past the death scene, they will

set that mental picture in their minds. They need to have alternative thoughts of happier times. To achieve this, you can introduce the technique called thought replacement.

Explain thought replacement to the participants after everyone has had the opportunity to share their positive memories. Expound on how they can continue to center their thoughts on good things, while at the same time they clear their minds of any painful, negative memories that haunt them. This is not to say that they should make saints of the deceased or revere them. But they can select their memories. They do not have to recall their loved ones as sick, in pain, and debilitated. They can, instead, recollect better times. They can use thought replacement. Suggest that their sharing of good times with the group is an example of positive thought replacement. These memories, and others like them, should be kept in mind and if necessary written down on a card that they carry with them. Whenever the gruesome memories come to mind, they should be a trigger for thought replacement. Instead of letting the unhappy thoughts continue, the participants can purposely start thinking of the memories they prefer and that more closely conform with the ways in which they knew the loved one.

The leader can generalize the thought replacement technique as something that can be used to create a more positive state of mind and develop more self-esteem. Whenever people feel overwhelmed and inept, they can reassure themselves of their skills and successes. They can build on their strengths.

3 Guilt

Guilt is common among the bereaved. It is one of the processes that takes place as they acknowledge the fact of the death of their loved ones. As they review the death and the relationship, they may be beset with If onlys and berate themselves for not doing more, better, or different. As the pain of grief subsides, so will the guilt.

It is a relief for the bereaved to be able to express their guilt, especially among people who understand and also feel guilt. Sometimes the group members have not confessed their guilt feelings to anyone because of shame and fear of criticism. When they do express them they often get quick reassurance. Unfortunately that does not always help, as this reassurance does not allow them to work through their guilt. They think the person did not really understand or was not paying attention.

People commonly feel guilty about anger and impatience that they may have felt during a long illness, about wishes to be relieved of the responsibility of caring for the sick person, or about not having been more aggressive in getting help. Some of the guilt feelings are based on reality, but more of them are exaggerated or stem from unrealistic expectations of themselves (Kushner, 1981). Nevertheless, the feelings are real.

Telling about guilt in the group is helpful because the participants can be more objective about the stated guilt of the other group members. They can see when they are asking too much of themselves, indulging in too much self-blame, and setting expectations that are unrealistic or totally impossible. This will help them more ably examine their own guilt. Some group members will report that they have no guilt and no regrets as they know they did all that they could do. These bereaved become role models and examples of the possibility that others can also look at what they did do, instead of only at what they did not do. Acceptance of themselves as human beings with limitations and of their relationship with the deceased person as a normal one that included ups and downs and irritations will assist them in being more understanding of themselves and their guilt feelings.

The facilitator and the group members cannot erase the guilt that the bereaved feel. It is easy, but not helpful, to say, "You do not have to feel guilty." The leader can be more understanding and set the tone for the group by saying, "It must be painful," or "It is hard to feel so responsible."

3b   Optional exercise or homework:

If time allows during the session, the group members can be asked to work on their guilt and their memories (see Table 5.6). They can share aloud or keep their thoughts to themselves after the exercise is completed. The questions in the exercise can be used to stimulate discussion. Or the participants can receive the topics in the form of a handout to work on at home.

4   Telephone buddies.

Let each participant select the name and telephone number of this week's telephone buddy.

5   Homework.

Encourage continued journal writing. You may assign the group exercise shown in Table 5.6 as homework. If so, be sure to discuss it during the next session.

6   Announcements.

Let the group know how many sessions are left and announce the topics. If they want special topics addressed, there is still time to suggest them.

7   One last thought:

Don't waste time in self-reproach. Forgive yourself immediately. Apologize to yourself, if necessary.

A note to the facilitator: Although there is no requirement that anyone attending the group has to talk, you may want to point out to the participants that the more they put into the group the more they will get out of it. As it is in life, so it is in the group.

Some of the participants will need more help than the group can provide. Sometimes they can be part of the group and get the needed individual help as well. Sometimes they are so needy that the group setting is not appropriate for them. Discuss the availability of one-to-one counseling with them privately before or after the meeting or by telephone.

This session is effective for all bereaved. Sharing memorabilia, discussing guilt, and learning thought replacement are invaluable for all ages and for anyone who is in grief.

Table 5.6   Guilt Exercise for Session Five

Think of your loved one while she or he was alive and answer the following questions. Write out your responses.

What do you wish you had done while your loved one was alive?

What did you do that pleases you or makes you proud?

What do you wish you had said?

What are you glad you said?

What do you miss the most?

What do you not miss?

What do you wish you had asked your loved one?

What did you discuss with your loved one that you are glad you talked about?

What do you think you can never do now?

What can you do now that you could not do while your loved one was alive?

What are your regrets?

What do you wish your loved one had done?

What will you never regret?

What did your loved one do that made you angry?

What did your loved one do that made you happy?

Table 5.7   Handout for Session Five

I'm not here
to offer answers
or to say
"It shouldn't have been
this way."
I'm here to listen,
to understand,
to simply be with you
when things are not
as you wish
they were.
Author Unknown

Table 5.8   Second Handout for Session Five

"Guilt, the gift that keeps on giving."—Erma Bombeck

"If we were intended to function with perfect hindsight, our eyeballs would be in the back of our heads."—Harriet Schiff

Guilt Management

1. Forgive yourself. This is more important than forgiving anyone else because you have to live with yourself.
2. Recognize guilt as part of the human condition. It is good when it inspires you to be a better person. It is excessive when you indulge in prolonged self-blame.
3. Get guilt out of your system by writing about it. This will also help you take a more objective view of it.
4. Talk about your guilt. Others will not be horrified.
5. Always remember that no one is perfect.
6. Do not drive yourself crazy with unanswerable Why? questions, and do not assume that you are so powerful that you have control over death.

SESSION SIX-COPING WITH LOSS

Topics

1 Review homework if an exercise was to be completed between sessions.
2 Past losses.
3 Coping.

Objectives

1 Participants will recognize how they have coped in the past.
2 Participants will identify positive coping skills.

Materials Needed

1 Name tags.
2 Sign-in sheet.
3 Slips of paper for names and telephone numbers.
4 A basket for the names and telephone numbers.
5 Handouts (see pages 113-114).
6 Table and chairs.
7 Refreshments.
8 Tissues.
9 Pencils for coping skills inventory.
10 Chalk or enamel board or flip chart.

Activities

1 Distribute name tags as the participants arrive, or have them pick them up next to the sign-in sheet.
2 Welcome the group members, and ask if anyone has a burning topic.
3 Homework from last session.
If the questions on guilt and the deceased were completed after the last session, take time to discuss them during this session.
4 Past losses.
Losses accumulate if they are not grieved over at the time they occur. They will complicate the present grief. If past losses were ignored, coping with the present loss is more difficult.
Everyone experiences many losses over a lifetime. They learn ways to cope with them that may be destructive or constructive. How they have coped with other losses is an indication of how they will cope with their present loss.

The purpose of discussing past losses is to determine the participants' coping strategies. Will what worked in the past work for them now? Do they need to learn other ways of coping with loss?

5   Coping.

Coping is a process and a technique. Coping can be good or bad, effective or ineffective, helpful or harmful. When a person is coping, they are struggling to deal with problems or difficulties. People can cope very well or have trouble coping. Any traumatic loss places great stress on an individual's coping skills.

The facilitator can develop an armamentarium of coping strategies. As the participants speak of past losses and how they responded to them, the leader can quietly make notes or openly write them on the chalk or enamel board or flip chart. It is not the facilitator's job, at this point, to sort out which coping methods are healthy or unhealthy. That can be saved for later discussion. Writing down the coping styles that the participants report suffices for now. All should be recorded without judgment.

Discussion of what works and what does not gives the participants a specific opportunity to help one another. They all want to cope well, and not all know how. They can learn from one another. Although what works for one group member may not work for another, they will still receive ideas. Also, the members will feel good about presenting ideas. They will feel more in control and more effective if they can suggest techniques that are working for them, and which may help someone else. Some participants will end up very pleased that they have learned new ways to cope. Others will be thrilled to learn that they are coping well.

Coping involves identifying the problem and/or the troublesome emotions. What specific problems need to be addressed? What uncomfortable emotions occur?

Problem-focused coping involves looking at what is happening in the environment and tackling the stressors. In problem-focused coping, individuals decide what people or events to avoid, whether they need to learn more to cope with the problem, whether others can be helpful or supportive, and whether new, fewer, or more activities are needed. The bereaved manipulate the environment to fit their needs. They seek information or advice, take specific problem-solving actions, or change activities to create new sources of satisfaction.

Emotion-focused coping deals with the reactions of the bereaved to events and situations. To cope with negative emotions, they may try looking at the situation from a different point of view, withdraw to work through their feelings, let off steam, discharge their emotions through crying, yelling, talking, or exercise, or simply remind themselves that time will help.

If the participants have difficulty identifying coping skills, the facilitator can help them by bringing up situations that they talked about in prior sessions or by giving typical examples such as those that follow.

What do you do when:

- You burst into tears in a room full of people?
- You feel that a repair person is taking advantage of you?

- You are faced with doing something that your loved one previously handled?
  - You feel lonely?
  - You cannot make a decision?
  - You feel insulted or left out?
  - People tell you how to live your life?
  - You are afraid?
  - You are worried about money?
  - You feel someone is using you?
  - Something you previously enjoyed no longer gives you pleasure?

If the facilitator has made notes on ways in which the group members have coped in the past, there will be answers to these questions, even if the bereaved seem overwhelmed by the enormity of present tasks. Reminders of good coping in the past will help them feel more confident in the present.

5a   Optional exercise:

The participants can be asked to do the coping skills inventory shown in Table 5.9 during the session. Alternatively, it can be discussed instead of individually assigned, or it can be given to them to do as homework.

6   Telephone buddies.

Each individual will draw the name and number of his or her telephone buddy for the week.

7   Homework.

Urge the group members to continue to write in their journals. This is a good coping mechanism, as it is an outlet for thoughts and feelings.

Suggest that they might want to set aside a time to grieve as a way to cope with their feelings of loss. To do this they pick a time and a place, and decide on how much time they want to put into grieving. They need to allow themselves at least one-half hour and no more than one and one-half hours. Each day at the designated time they are to go to their grieving place and think about their loss for the chosen amount of time. When the time is up, they are to remove themselves from this place and get busy on some activity, project, or exercise.

8   Announcements.

Let the participants know that there are two more sessions. Announce the topics. Remind them that they may also request subjects that interest them.

9   One last thought:

> "Sometimes our fate resembles a fruit tree in winter. Who would think that those branches would turn green again and blossom, but we hope it, we know it."—Johann Goethe

A note to the facilitator: Start making plans for the participants who need more support or professional help than a time-limited group can provide. The facilitator will want to make announcements in the group, distribute brochures and handouts about other available groups, and talk privately to group members who need more intensive help. It is not unusual for people who are going through a normal grief reaction to need more support. Some of the group members' problems will necessitate skilled assistance. Pay particular attention to the following:

1   Mental health problems.

Clinical depression, which differs from normal grief in that the affected individuals

cannot be cheered up

feel they cannot do anything right

see themselves as useless and in the way

feel hopeless and helpless

feel and appear empty

are irritable rather than openly angry

are depressed even when good things happen

Suicidal or homicidal ideation.

Have specific plans to kill themselves or others.

Breaks with reality—hallucinations, illusions, delusions.

Anxiety, panic attacks, phobias.

Substance abuse.

2   Maladaptive grief—delayed, exaggerated, enshrinement, inhibited, masked.

3   Debilitating physical problems.

4   More new and traumatic changes than one can reasonably handle at one time.

5   Needs for tangible help such as money, transportation, or a place to live.

To determine the extent of the problem, the facilitator may ask questions such as,

Have you ever had this problem before?

What did you do about it?

What helped?

What have you tried now? What has worked?

Always respect the individuals' right to confidentiality and their preferences when making a referral.

The topic of coping is excellent for anyone who has experienced the loss of a loved one.

Table 5.9   Coping Skills Inventory for Session Six

When you have problems and are under stress, which of the following coping mechanisms do you use? Check all that you have used or are using. Then go back over the list and note which of your coping methods are constructive and which are destructive. Make plans to replace the destructive and dangerous techniques with more positive ones. What coping skills do you have that are not on the list? Add them.

1. Work on projects that take concentration.
2. Buy something.
3. Go to bed.
4. Drink alcohol or take mind-altering drugs.
5. Talk about it with others.
6. Read up on the problem.
7. Lose yourself in a good book.
8. Become physically ill.
9. Get professional help.
10. Blame someone.
11. Fix what is broken.
12. Put it out of your mind.
13. Eat more, or less.
14. Exercise.
15. Rant, rave, and curse.
16. Stick to a schedule.
17. Go for a walk.
18. Cry.
19. Try to look at the bright side.
20. Try to see the humor in the situation.
21. Pray.
22. Meditate.
23. Look for other options or alternatives.
24. Say no.
25. Try something else.
26. Blame yourself.
27. Find an expert to help.
28. Tackle the problem and get it out of the way.
29. Put it off.
30. Problem solve.
31. Ignore it.
32. Take a chance.
33. Accept it.
34. Hope for a miracle.
35. Escape.
36. Daydream.
37. Wait to see what will happen.
38. Keep it to yourself.
39. Find something else to do.
40. Work at your hobby.
41. Write.
42. Give yourself a treat.
43. Become moody.
44. Play with your pet.
45. Sit in a hot tub.
46. Hope for the best.
47. Expect the worst.
48. Get more information.
49. Analyze the problem.
50. Do something for someone else.
51. Listen to music.
52. Get a massage.
53. Work on a puzzle.
54. Watch television.
55. Go to the movies.
56. Live for today.
57. Correct mistakes.
58. Figure out what you want.
59. Clean house.
60. Mow the lawn.
61. Get on the telephone.
62. Talk to yourself.
63. Sing.
64. Pretend everything is all right.
65. Put it off.

No coping mechanism is all bad. None is all good. Some will give short-term help. Some will help in the long run. None will help everyone all of the time. You will develop your own list of coping skills that work for you.

Table 5.10   Handout for Session Six

The book *Quick Fixes: 303 Ways to Help Yourself Before the Therapist Arrives* outlines the following steps to problem solving.
1. Pinpoint the problem.
    Define the problem. What are you worrying about? Is action required?
2. Know your goal.
    What do you want to achieve?
3. Look for solutions.
    Write down any possible solution. Brainstorm. Include the impractical and outrageous.
4. Analyze the advantages and disadvantages of every solution you wrote down.
    List all the advantages and disadvantages of each approach.
5. Decide on an approach.
    Does the approach lead you to accomplish your goal? Pick the easiest approach with the fewest complications.
6. Put the approach into action.
7. Keep evaluating.
    If the approach does not work, or if you do not like it, you can change it.

You can't control the length of your life, but you can control its width and depth. You can't control the contour of your face, but you can control the expression. You can't control the weather, but you can control the atmosphere of your mind. Why worry about things you can't control, when you can keep yourself busy controlling the things that depend on you.—Author unknown

Table 5.11   Second Handout for Session Six

Comes the Dawn
After a while you learn the subtle difference
Between holding a hand and chaining a soul,
And you learn that love doesn't mean leaning
And company doesn't mean security,
And you begin to understand that kisses aren't contracts
And presents aren't promises
And you begin to accept your defeats
With your head held high and your eyes open,
With the grace of an adult, not the grief of a child.
You learn to build your roads
On today because tomorrow's ground
Is too uncertain for plans, and futures have
A way of falling down in midflight.
After awhile you learn that even sunshine
Burns if you get too much,
So you plan your own garden and decorate
Your own soul, instead of waiting
For someone to bring you flowers.
And you learn that you really can endure,
That you really are strong
And you really do have worth
And you learn and learn . . . and you learn
With every goodbye you learn
(Author unknown; qtd. in Farra, 1986).

SESSION SEVEN-GRIEF AND ANGER

Topics

1 Review of homework if coping inventory was to be completed after the last session.
2 Report on coping skills used, including the grieving time technique.
3 Anger (Schiff, 1986).

Objectives

1 The participants will understand their feelings of anger.
2 The participants will learn techniques for managing their anger.

Materials Needed

1 Name tags.
2 Sign-in sheet.
3 Slips for names and telephone numbers.
4 A basket to hold the name and telephone number slips.
5 Materials for the written exercise.
6 Handouts (see pages 118-119).
7 Table and chairs.
8 Refreshments.
9 Tissues.
10 Chalk or enamel board or flip chart.

Activities

1 Welcome everyone. Report on those who could not attend. Follow up on ongoing concerns. Ask if there are any issues that need to be discussed right now.
2 Follow up on homework, coping skills used, group members' experience with using the technique of a grieving time.
3 Anger.
Anger is the feeling of outrage and indignation at someone or something. Anger is a normal reaction to real or imagined wrongs. Anger is a feeling (Tavris, 1982), and feelings are neither right or wrong. They are just feelings. The group members need to look at how feelings are handled. Anger is part of the normal grief reaction. It is part of the healing feelings of mourning.
The facilitator may ask,

- How many have ever felt anger?
- How many feel some anger now?

- How many feel no anger now?
- How many are comfortable with their anger?
- How many are uncomfortable with their anger?

Because there are some common themes of anger in the bereaved, the facilitator may ask,
Who is angry at or about

- medical care?
- congregation, clergy, God?
- the deceased?
- friends, relatives, neighbors?
- the funeral director?
- anything else?

Explain that these are all common targets for anger. If the facilitator has examples of such anger in his or her personal experience, it is appropriate to share them. Anger at God and at the deceased may seem unacceptable to some of the bereaved even as they feel it, but actual anecdotes will allow them to admit to their feelings and free them to be able to deal with them (Freeman, 1990).

Anger at the deceased can be related to feelings of abandonment, loss of hope that the relationship could someday get better, a secret affair or scandal that was revealed after the death or on the deathbed, lack of preparation or provisions for the survivor, or feelings that the deceased neglected him or herself and contributed to an untimely death.

Depending on the size and tenor of the group, the facilitator may encourage ventilation of the group members' anger or ask them to write out what has angered and irritated them and how they have handled it. After the written exercise, they can be asked to share their thoughts and feelings. Ventilation in the group is helpful and therapeutic. People will find that others accept their anger, that others have similar gripes, and that airing their anger makes them better able to deal with it. It is a supportive experience because their feelings are accepted nonjudgmentally.

Much of the anger will be justified and will be encouraged. None of the anger will be labeled as wrong. Hear the group out. Ask for suggestions on what to do about specific circumstances. If action is called for, promote it. If nothing can be done about the anger, look at ways the participants can use it for their own benefit. If the anger is apparently harmful to the bereaved, ask for suggestions on ways to manage or dispel it.

Always ask the following:

- What have others told you to do? (Everybody, it seems, tries to give the bereaved helpful advice.)
- What have you done so far?
- What have you done in the past?
- What has worked?
- What seems to have made it worse?

The participants should be able to leave the group with feelings of relief, acceptance, understanding, and some control. They may have been able to find some humor in their anger, determine ways to handle it, and see some positives in it.

4   Telephone buddies.

Have all the participants draw the name and number of their telephone buddy for the week.

5   Homework.

Ask the group members to think about personal short- and long-term goals. That will be the topic for the eighth and last formal support group session.

Suggest that they continue to write in their journals.

Ask them to continue to experiment with a grieving time.

6   Announcements.

Remind the group that the next session will be the last. However, the facilitator may want to plan an informal ninth session. This helps the group say good-bye. It should be a social situation, lunch in a restaurant, a potluck in the regular meeting place, a party in a participant's home, or whatever the group members suggest. Start planning the time, place, and structure of a get-together, or ask the participants to think about it and let their preferences be known in the next session.

7   One last thought:

> "Holding on to anger is like grasping a hot coal with the intent of throwing it at someone else—you are the one who gets burned."—Buddha

A note to the facilitator: The facilitator may want to summarize what has been covered so far and point out how far the group has come.

Anger is a viable topic for all bereaved, but even more so for the survivors whose loved ones died untimely or violent deaths. This session can be presented to them without alterations.

Table 5.12   Handout for Session Seven

Managing Anger

1. Recognize that you are angry.
2. Talk to yourself about your anger. You may be justifiably angry, but choose not to act on your feelings.
3. Make a statement about your anger, to yourself or to the person who angers you.
4. Do not make threatening remarks to other people. Do not put them on the defensive.
5. Count to ten—or one hundred.
6. Decide to not carry a grudge because it is to your advantage to be free of it.
7. Think how you would like to be treated. Treat others in that manner.
8. Do not take your anger at one person or situation out on another person or situation.
9. Work out your anger on physical endeavors.
10. Write out your anger.
11. Fantasize what you would like to do, but do not do it.
12. Use cold courtesy, i.e., "I beg your pardon."
13. Decide to discuss it at a later time.
14. Do not incite yourself.
15. Use humor.
16. Defuse anger by staying calm.
17. Try to see the other person's point of view.
18. Decide if it is worth your anger.
19. Use anger to motivate yourself to do something about it.
20. Talk it out with fellow sufferers.
21. Pretend it is happening to someone else.
22. Admit mistakes (Hughes, 1993).

Table 5.13   Second Handout for Session Seven

Wouldn't this be a wonderful world if folks who lost their tempers never found them again?—B. Bader

Everyone has problems in some area of self-control. If you try your best, that's the important thing.—Daniel A. Sugerman Ph.D.

Two things a man should never be angry at: what he can help, and what he cannot help.—Daniel A. Sugerman Ph.D.

You'll be able to change things faster if you criticize deeds and not people. —Daniel A. Sugerman Ph.D.

Names can hurt a lot. If you can't resist using them, at least try good ones.—Daniel A. Sugerman Ph.D.

The real secret of patience is to find something else to do in the meantime.—Dell Pencil Puzzles and Word Games

If you are patient in one moment of anger, you will escape a hundred days of sorrow.—Chinese proverb

A man's car stalled in the heavy traffic as the light turned green. All his efforts to start the engine failed, and a chorus of honking behind him made matters worse. He finally got out of his car and walked back to the first driver. "I'm very sorry," he said, "but I can't seem to get my car started. If you'll go up there and give it a try, I'll stay here and blow your horn for you."—Sunshine Magazine

SESSION EIGHT-GRIEVING AND GROWING

Topics

1 Goals.
2 Identifying strengths.

Objective

1 The participants will look at how far they have come and at where they want to go.

Materials Needed

1 Name tags.
2 Sign-in sheet.
3 Slips for names and telephone numbers.
4 A basket to hold the name and telephone number slips.
5 Paper and pencils for the written exercise.
6 Table and chairs.
7 Handouts (see pages 123-125).
8 Tissues.
9 Evaluation forms.
10 Refreshments.
11 Chalk or enamel board or flip chart.

Activities

1 Welcome.
Ask for any topics that need to be covered during this last session. Some important subjects may be suggested. If that is the case, devote more time to them and less to goal setting. If there is no time to discuss what is on the planned agenda, distribute the goal setting handout shown in Table 5.14, so that the group members can work on goals on their own time.
2 Goals.
To determine goals the group members may want to think back to some of the earlier sessions and identify where they are in the grief process. They may also want to look at how they label themselves. For example,

- Do they think of themselves as widowed, married, single?
- What do they call themselves? Mrs. John Smith? Mary Smith?
- Do they say "I" or "we"?
- What have they done about their wedding and engagement rings?
- How far ahead to they look?

There are no right or wrong answers, but there are many differences in the ways that people manage themselves in regard to symbols and thoughts of marriage. Some well-adjusted widowed people always wear their wedding rings and think of themselves as married. Others immediately start establishing a separate identity. The group members will learn from one another and receive support from one another.

Some of the group participants will not be able to look ahead and set goals for the day, much less for tomorrow, next week, or a year from now. To do so is, nevertheless, a worthwhile exercise because it helps them see that they can exert some control in their lives.

The goals are valuable because

- There is a sense of accomplishment when they reach their goal.
- They can see actual progress.
- They give the bereaved something tangible, a direction, that provides structure to a life in which they feel cast adrift.
- Working toward something and finishing the project helps relieve stress.
- Goals can be things that they look forward to doing.

Goals do not have to be major or long term. They can be short term ones, such as backing the car down the driveway, setting aside fifteen minutes a day to go through papers or pictures, making one phone call tomorrow, going to the grocery store, or answering one letter. The goal may be not worrying ahead, concentrating on getting through one day, or getting to the barber or the beauty parlor.

Group members may think of long-term goals, such as making new friends, going back to school, or taking a trip. The facilitator may have to provide some clues to get them started. Because the leader has heard of some of the members' concerns over the eight weeks, he or she may be able to make personal suggestions or ask if they might want to consider one pursuit or another.

The facilitator, with the help of all the group, will also want each participant to recognize the apparent changes he or she has made during the short duration of the group. Moods will be brighter, more optimism will be expressed, group members will have done things that made them proud of themselves, decisions will have been made. They will have succeeded in achieving some personal goals.

The leader will want to ask the group to work at writing their goals and accomplishments, so that they will have a positive motivator to refer to when they need some encouragement.

Along with the goal setting, ask the participants to list 10 things they liked to do in the past or like to do now. Have them star the ones they can do alone and circle the ones that cost less than $5.00. Suggest that they include some of these activities when they do their goal setting.

3 Strengths.

The topic of individual strengths blends into the discussion of goals. The participants will be pointing out what they and the others have already accomplished and giving one another hope for what else they can do. Help the group members give to one another by reminding their fellow members of what they have survived and what problems they have already tackled. Make sure that every participant hears at least one good thing about himself or herself. Ask them to write their strengths on their paper, so they can remind themselves of their abilities when they feel less competent. This is a good time for the group members to look at how they felt when they came to the group and how they feel now. Some participants will demonstrate dramatic differences that will be noticed by everyone in the group. Everyone receives the gift of hearing that they have worked hard and well, faced their situation, and made discernible progress.

    4   Telephone buddies.

Have each participant draw the name and number of a telephone buddy one last time.

    5   Homework.

Urge them to continue to do well.

    6   Announcements.

If a social session is to follow, complete plans for it.

Let the group members know when the next eight-session support group will be held. They are invited to attend if they want to repeat the series then or at any other time. Let them know about other support groups that are available in the community.

Request that they complete their evaluation of the sessions and hand it in before they leave.

    7   One last thought: Within every good-bye is a new hello.

A note to the facilitator: The purpose of the evaluation (Table 5.15) is to provide feedback about the effectiveness of the support group. Alter the example shown to include any information that you or your organization wants to know or measure.

This session, more than any of the others, is geared to the widowed. It can, however, be adapted to other kinds of losses. Because roles are always confusing after a loved one dies, the same type of questions about roles can be asked of parents, siblings, or friends. How do they describe and define themselves? Do they continue to think of themselves as parents since the death of the child? Setting goals, identifying strengths, and noting progress are excellent subjects and will be profitably discussed by anyone who has been through a life-altering trauma.

The goal-setting handout is more appropriate for the widowed but can be used with anyone if questions 1 and 4 are eliminated.

Table 5.14   Handout for Session Eight

Goals

1. I am most worried about (circle choices) health, money, repairs, yard maintenance, relationships, transportation, paper work, self-care, learning new skills, jobs
my loved one previously managed, e.g., homemaking, finances, car maintenance,
making decisions, other.

2. List the items circled under the appropriate heading:

I CAN DO   NEED EXPERT HELP   CAN BE PUT OFF

3. Set goals for the items in the I CAN DO and NEED EXPERT HELP columns. Put
items in the CAN BE PUT OFF column in the "to-do-when-time-and-energy-allow"
category.

WHAT I CAN DO TODAY.

WHAT I CAN DO TOMORROW.

WHAT CAN BE DONE A LITTLE AT A TIME.

WHAT I CAN DO NEXT WEEK.

WHAT I CAN DO NEXT MONTH.

WHAT NEEDS TO BE ADDRESSED BY SPECIALISTS.

WHERE I CAN GET THE NEEDED ASSISTANCE.

WHAT I NEED TO DO TO FIND EXPERT HELP.

WHEN I WILL APPROACH THE EXPERTS FOR ASSISTANCE.

4. Some things I want to do for myself that I did not have the time or opportunity to
do before (circle choices): school, travel, buying something new, new skills, hobbies,
volunteering, paid employment, writing, friends, family, clubs, gardening, sports,
activism for a cause, other.
List those that are circled under the following headings:

CAN START TODAY   NEED FURTHER STUDY   FUTURE PROJECTS

5. Set goals for the entries listed in the CAN START TODAY and NEED FURTHER
STUDY columns. Keep a list of the items in the FUTURE PROJECTS column for future
reference when time and energy allow.

Table 5.14   Handout for Session Eight *(Continued)*

Goals

WHAT I CAN DO TODAY.

WHAT I NEED TO RESEARCH.

WHAT I CAN DO A LITTLE AT A TIME.

6. Make three lists. One the first, write how you spend your time now. On the second, write how you would like to spend your time. On the third, write how you plan to be spending your time a year from now.

HOW I SPEND MY TIME

HOW I WOULD LIKE TO SPEND MY TIME

HOW I PLAN TO SPEND MY TIME A YEAR FROM NOW

7. What do you have to do to be able to spend your time as you want to?

WHAT CAN YOU DO TODAY?

WHAT CAN YOU DO IN THE FUTURE?

WHAT CAN YOU DO A LITTLE AT A TIME?

8. As you determine what you want to do or need to do, you can set short- or long-term goals. Part of goal setting is deciding your approaches. Each step toward your goal is an accomplishment that leads you closer to what you want to achieve. This is all part of being in control and getting what you want out of life.

Happiness is not a matter of good fortune or worldly possessions. It is a mental attitude. It comes from appreciating what we have instead of being miserable about what we don't have. It's so simple—yet so hard for the human mind to comprehend. —Author unknown.

Table 5.15   Evaluation Form

Group facilitator _____ Date _____

1. The group was   a. helpful   b. not very helpful
Comments:

2. The length of each session was   a. too short   b. too long   c. just right
Comments:

3. The number of sessions was   a. too few   b. too many   c. just right
Comments:

4. The subject matter was   a. what I needed   b. not what I needed
Comments:

5. The location of the group was   a. convenient   b. inconvenient
Comments:

6. The room was   a. comfortable   b. uncomfortable
Comments:

7. What was most helpful to you?

8. What was least helpful to you?

9. Do you have any suggestions for change?

CONCLUSION

Structured bereavement support groups are very satisfying to facilitators who have limited time and busy schedules and to the bereaved who like beginnings and endings and who are also occupied with other responsibilities. They are a good approach for people who are generally uncomfortable in groups, as the group members soon feel secure because of the similarity of the problems and the reassurance of seeing the same people each session. Participants and facilitators alike will feel more in control in time-limited groups because they are more predictable.

Chapter 6

Unstructured Bereavement Support Groups

Unstructured bereavement groups are open-ended support groups. This means that participants may come and go as they want. They may be unstructured also in that anyone in any stage of grief, after any type of loss, is eligible to attend. Such groups occur and function and apparently fill a need. There are unstructured groups, however, that meet to serve individuals in specialized categories of grief. Although people may come and go as they please, they have to meet the single criterion of having experienced a particular type of loss, such as the loss of a child, parent, spouse, sibling, or friend. The loss can be further defined as one resulting from suicide, murder, or drunk drivers, or from traumatic incidents, such as war, fire, tornado, earthquake, or any localized catastrophe. Besides relationship to the deceased and cause of death, there may be other screening measures, such as length of time since the loss occurred, age of the participants, and whether the bereaved have problems that can be appropriately addressed by the group. An unstructured group made up of bereaved of all ages, with various kinds of losses, will have problems based on comparison and competition and the feeling that others do not understand because their losses are so different. These can be overcome through the facilitator's intervention. The leader can state that any loss is the worst loss when it is our loss and that all losses are followed by grief. The group members will learn to accommodate differences and will learn from them, but the group is more effective and easier to manage when there is similarity among the members.

The major characteristic of an unstructured group is that it has no beginning and end. It meets regularly at a set place and time. The leader or leaders always appear. There is no time commitment by the participants. They may decide to attend steadily over a period of time, attend sporadically, or show up once and never return.

ADVANTAGES

Flexible attendance   The advantage of the ongoing unstructured bereavement support group is that people can attend when they want to. If they miss one session, they can make it to the next session. There is always group support available. There is no urgency about getting everything into a few sessions, as there is in a closed-end group. The bereaved can take care of other things that come up in their lives and then go back to the group. If they miss some sessions, they have not missed out. They can live their lives and work the group in when they can, whereas with a closed-end group, participants must work their lives around the group.

More roles available   An open-end group offers people the opportunity to become more than a bereaved participant. The group members can develop other roles for themselves as mentors for the newly bereaved, as role models, or as assistants in the running of the group. They can spearhead social activities and be responsible for mingling opportunities after the support group sessions. When there is a regular meeting place after each support group session, those who no longer need formal discussion in a guided group setting can drop in for the social aspects without attending the support group. They can continue to be a part of the group in a way that is meaningful to them and is not disruptive to those who have more pressing emotional needs. Graduate volunteers can do follow-up on participants who have dropped out of the group. They can assist the leader when the bereaved become so upset that they need to withdraw from the group. One volunteer can be responsible for accompanying them, being with them during their distress, and encouraging them to rejoin the group.

Because participants in ongoing groups are frequently at varying stages in the grief process, the newly bereaved can be encouraged by the progress they see in those who have been bereaved longer, who have been through what they are going through and are surviving. By the same token, those who have been bereaved for a longer period feel more hopeful about themselves when they see that they have passed the stage of acute grief that is displayed by the more newly bereaved.

Although group members in closed-end groups develop friendships, there is more opportunity for making new friends and adjusting to a new social scene in long-term, ongoing groups. Participants can exercise their social skills in a protected setting with others who are also reaching out for a social life. Close relationships develop because there is time and opportunity.

Another advantage of an open-end group is that it gives the group facilitator and the sponsoring organization a chance to test the waters. The group may begin by being open to everyone in grief because the numbers of people needing bereavement support are unknown. From this the facilitator learns what specialized groups are needed.

DISADVANTAGES

Constant recruitment   Unstructured bereavement support groups need a lot of maintenance. Publicity has to be ongoing, so that people know the group is out there and available to them. If new participants are not recruited, the group becomes stale, boring, and personality clashes occur. The same people saying and doing the same things over many weeks gets on everyone's nerves, and bickering breaks out. The result is that more time is spent working through differences and hurt feelings than is put into bereavement support.

If new participants are not recruited and the group members like each other, as often happens, the group evolves into a social group. Because the people become mutually supportive, enjoy each other, focus on their day-to-day lives, develop inside jokes, and see each other frequently outside the group, new people cannot break in. Someone who comes to the group for bereavement support will find the participants involved in one another's ongoing activities and acting happy and cheerful. The newcomers will feel left out, will find the group too jolly for their moods and needs, and will not come back. If there is not a constant influx of newly bereaved, the group will coalesce; it will be a support group but not what the newly bereaved are looking for (Folken, 1991).

If new participants are joining the group on a regular basis, the members will be attuned to that. The members who have reached a different phase in their grief process will drop out or move on. Those who remain will continue to address the issues of adjusting to a world without the presence of their loved ones.

Consequently, any unstructured bereavement support group will need mechanisms to ensure that the group meets the objectives for which it was founded. There will have to be a source of new referrals. Affiliation with a hospice, hospital, or funeral home can provide such a source. Sporadic publicity is helpful, but the group's availability must be constantly before the public so that people who need a support group can find it when they need it. Also, without ongoing recruitment, attendance will drop and the group will become less viable if only three or four attend each time. With such low participation, people lose heart. If one or two miss a session, there is no group.

Termination   Group participants who do not want to leave the group, but who have advanced beyond it, can graduate to other groups or other responsibilities. There may be a social group, a transition group, or a way for an individual to stay involved by taking on some responsibility for the program, such as handling publicity, playing host or hostess, becoming a coleader, or serving as a role model for the newly bereaved. The person may have expertise that is valuable for the bereaved, such as financial, security, medical, or legal knowledge.

Leaving an ongoing bereavement support group is difficult because the group does not stop; the bereaved who have outgrown the group may be reluctant to leave because of attachments and habit. They must be encouraged to move on to other, more-suitable groups, or into an official category as an assistant or specialist, or the group will grow stagnant and disband.

Because people do come and go in open-end groups, all the participants will have seen examples of participants' leaving the group. This is a constant reminder that there are beginnings and endings (Yalom, 1985).

Goal setting helps with the problem of termination. When one's goals are achieved, it is time to leave the group. If goals are not set, or if they are vague, there can still be the subjective knowledge of feeling well and managing successfully. If there are new activities, relationships, and pleasures, the facilitators and the other group members can congratulate the participants on their apparent progress, wish them well, and help them move on.

Facilitators' commitment   Leading an ongoing support group is a major undertaking. If the group is to be facilitated by one person, that person is obligated to be there each time the group convenes, have a plan for each meeting, find substitute leaders during vacation and sick leave, and be able to manage attendees who need more than the group can offer, who need to move on, or who are inappropriate for the group. If participants are to be screened, this same person must have the flexibility to do that on a timely basis. The leader must also line up coleaders or have someone readily available to help when needed. Auxiliary help to take care of the many arrangements is nice to have and sometimes essential.

Group size   The size of this kind of group cannot readily be controlled. As mentioned previously, the group can be too small to function well, but it can also be too large and become unwieldy. The solution for this is to create more groups or to address the total group on an educational basis, breaking up into smaller groups for discussion. But each smaller group needs someone to take responsibility for leading it. This not only means coleaders but additional help, as well. Can such help be found among the group members?

STRUCTURE

Schedule of meetings   Sometimes weekly meetings do not seem feasible because space and personnel are not available. Although the bereaved may do fine with meetings every other week or even once a month, an open-end group needs a regular schedule. If meetings do not occur weekly, in the same place, and with the same facilitator, prospective participants become discouraged. The week that they can attend may be just the week that the group does not meet. The newly bereaved welcome weekly support. Without regular meetings, those looking for a group may find figuring out the schedule too complicated and give up. If one time a week is set aside for the group meeting, it fits into the rhythm of the participants' lives. They know that every week at a certain time the meeting will take place. That time can be reserved without thinking or planning. Nor should the group ever be canceled; that is the reason why a coleader, or someone to substitute, is crucial.

It is best to always hold the group at the same location unless a permanent move to a new site is necessary. Meeting in different places, such as participants' homes or the home base of a speaker, or scheduling a social event somewhere else on a meeting night is poor policy because it deters new members from following through on joining. It is hard enough to walk in on an established group without having to track it down. Remember that it is pain that drives the bereaved to seek support. A scavenger hunt for the meeting place increases anxiety and destroys motivation.

Length of meetings   Ongoing groups should start and end on time, just as closed-end groups do. The length of each session is established by the leader. A one hour meeting is as short as the facilitator can reasonably make it. If a speaker and refreshments are planned, a group can meet for two or two and one-half hours, and that is long enough for any group session.

Programming for the meetings   Scheduling a speaker occasionally enhances the vitality of the group. Allow time for discussion after each presentation. Do not worry about repeat performances. Since it is expected that there will always be new group members, there will always be new people to hear the speech. The bereaved will also receive the same information in different ways at different stages in their grief process. Set up a yearly schedule, with speakers once a month, special topics or exercises once a month, and participant discussion the rest of the time. Having a regular format is easier for the leaders because they do not have to scurry each week to find something to do to keep the group going and stimulated. Once effective speakers and exercises are found, they can be rescheduled on a regular basis. Leaders should not let something good get away.

The following is a list of topics that are helpful to the bereaved:

1 Planning ahead
2 Intimacy and sexuality
3 Health insurance
4 Sharing a home
5 The new identity
6 Loneliness
7 Social situations
8 Making decisions
9 Techniques for dealing with grief
10 Anxiety and fear
11 Sadness and regret
12 Insecurity
13 Anger
14 Guilt
15 Hope
16 Developing support
17 Physical stress and health
18 Complicated grief
19 Enhancing self-esteem
20 Depression
21 Attitudes
22 Taking responsibility
23 Who am I?
24 Stress management
25 New life-styles
26 Is life fair?
27 New beginnings
28 Financial management
29 Home and personal security
30 Taking risks
31 Living one day at a time
32 Goal setting
33 Identifying strengths
34 Surviving single
35 Finding and accepting help
36 Helping others to help yourself
37 Dealing with fatigue and lack of energy
38 Nutrition

39   Relaxation
40   Humor that helps
41   Small pleasures
42   Assertiveness
43   Consumer protection
44   Shopping and cooking for one
45   Coping with the holidays
46   The dating scene
47   Remarriage
48   In-laws and other relatives
49   Paid employment
50   Living wills
51   Estate planning
52   Home maintenance
53   Housing options
54   Social skills
55   Traveling alone
56   Entertaining alone

All of these topics are useful for widowed persons groups, and most are appropriate for other groups as well. Specialized loss groups will want to add other topics, such as,

57   The needs of surviving children
58   Talking to children
59   Helping children in grief while you are grieving
60   Why suicide?
61   Legal issues
62   Finding help for grieving children
63   Understanding children's grief
64   The police investigation
65   When it doesn't make sense
66   Asking why
67   Who needs you?
68   What to say to others

The facilitator can also use topics from the list to promote discussions. The leader can make a very short presentation and explore some aspects of the subject, ask questions, and then open up the topic for discussion.

Group exercises provide variety and help focus a group. They may be used as an introduction to a theme, as an ice-breaker, as a diversion, or as the focal point of the meeting's agenda. None of the following exercises are original. They have been passed around among group leaders, discussed in conferences, experienced in workshops, described in journals, and redesigned by hordes of facilitators. Although I cannot give credit to the unknown originators of these activities, neither can I claim credit for having thought of them myself.

Feeling Good Exercises

Helping others   Ask everyone present to rate their mood from 1 to 10, with 10 being the highest rating. Meet briefly with those with the highest mood ratings. Suggest ways in which they can cheer up the participants with the lowest ratings. Ask them to listen, to suggest alternative thoughts, to point out some good things that are happening, to tell a joke, to smile. After 10 to 15 minutes, ask for updated mood assessments. Check on what raised and what lowered the ratings. What worked? What did not? How did the group members who had responsibility for cheering up others feel about the task? Did it make them feel better or worse?

Strength identification   Ask each group member to write down two or three things they did during the week that made them feel good, made them proud, or were accomplishments. Then direct the group to circulate, everyone making a point of talking one-to-one to everyone else as they exchange accomplishments. Afterward they review their proud and pleasant moments with the entire group, along with their responses to the exercise. How can they use what they just did to help themselves feel better and increase their self-esteem?

Pollyanna   Everybody writes down one thing that made them unhappy, displeased, or disappointed. Going around the circle, each participant presents an incident to the group. The group members suggest positive ways to feel about the situation or possible good that might result from it. Encourage brainstorming and ridiculous ideas. They can be farfetched. Humor is great. Laughing and crying at the same time is totally acceptable. Ask later for the participants' reactions. Was there resentment and anger? Was there relief? Was there a broadening of perspective?

Compliments   One group member is in the "hot seat." Everyone else in the group says one nice thing to him or her. Go around the circle until everyone has the opportunity to be in the hot seat. The facilitator, or a designated person, will make a list of the compliments given to each participant.

Uniqueness and Universalities Exercises

Lemon exercise   Pass a bowl of lemons. Each participant picks one and becomes well acquainted with it, memorizing identifying characteristics. The lemons are returned to the bowl. Then everyone is asked to retrieve his or her lemon. Ask the participants to conjecture on the moral of this exercise. Is it that everyone is unique? That no one should be labeled? That all have good and bad characteristics? That we can become attached to someone or something once we accept what it, he, or she is? Is it that getting to know someone is part of the pleasure and the process? Any response is fine.

Past In 5 minutes, tell what experiences made you what you are today. End with a peak experience that made you feel great. Go around the circle.

Favorite things Name three things you like to do. Resolve to do one of them during the week. Report back to the group next week.

Dyads Ask the group to pair off. Each participant tells one other participant about the death of the loved one. Allow about 5 minutes. Then each pair gets together with another pair. The person who heard about the other's loss introduces him or her to the other pair. Allow about 10 minutes. Instruct the quartet to meet with four other people and repeat the process. Increase the time allotted to allow all eight to speak. Keep increasing the number and pairing with an equal number until the pairs become the entire group. Then open up discussion by asking for similarities and differences.

Any of the group exercises suggested for the closed-end bereavement support group can also be used in an open-end group.

PROCEDURE

Introductions Because it is hoped that new members will enter the group on a regular basis, you need a procedure for ensuring the orderly introduction of additional participants. The newcomers need recognition and attention to their concerns and questions, and they need to learn the ways of the group. To this end, everyone already in the group should be prepared to follow a prearranged procedure for incorporating others into the group. New members complete an informational fact sheet prior to or after the meeting. The old members can be linked with telephone buddies to the new members and check with them between meetings. But the new arrivals must be acclimated to the group through an introductory process that helps them identify with the rest of the participants and feel as though they have come to the right place. This is accomplished through a therapeutic procedure in which all the participants, old and new, say who they are and why they attend the support group. This is to be short—two or three sentences that explain their loss and need for support.

Rules After the introductions, when some of the anxiety has lessened, the leader or one of the regular participants recites the rules of the group.

The major rule, of course, is confidentiality. Other rules might include the sharing of air time so that one person does not monopolize the group, the precedence of pressing problems, and stopping and starting on time.

In each group meeting, or at least every now and then, the group leader will want to include a question that it is appropriate to ask each participant. This device enables the facilitator to go around the circle and elicit the ideas, experiences, and feelings of each person. It is a technique for including those participants who do not have much to say. It helps them become more comfortable in speaking to the group and helps the other group members get to know them.

EVALUATION

Timing   Evaluation by consumers is as helpful in open-end groups as it is in closed-end groups. The problem is in deciding when to do it, since there is no convenient ending time to ask for an assessment of the bereavement support series. The leaders have to decide not only when to evaluate, but what to evaluate. If speakers are used, there might be an evaluation after each presentation (see Table 6.1).

Evaluating a guest speaker's presentation is fairly clear-cut. Such is not the case when members are asked to evaluate the effectiveness of an ongoing support group. Some participants may have just begun and may be uncertain as to what they can expect; they may be unsure whether the group can meet their needs. Others may have been there for some time and want something other than what the group can provide. They may be looking for a social life, a mate, or specific guidance about a tangible problem. In either of these instances the evaluation responses will be discouraging to the leader. So how does a group facilitator pick a time for evaluations? The leader can arbitrarily pick an evaluation date every quarter. An evaluation can also be sent to anyone who attends the group and does not return. Participants might also be asked to complete an evaluation after they have attended for two or three months (see Table 6.2)

Need for information on effectiveness   The leaders need to know whether the bereavement support group is more than just a nice idea. Are the leaders and the group process helpful? Are they effective? This will be indicated by the evaluations that the group participants complete when they rate speakers. Positive evaluations of their support group experiences attest that the recipients of the services were satisfied and that they benefitted. If they would recommend the support groups to friends, one may infer that they felt good about what happened to them. These reports are subjective but valid.

Table 6.1   Speaker Evaluation Form

Speaker _____ Date _____

Topic _____

1. Did the presentation meet your expectations?
   Yes _____
   No _____
   Somewhat _____
   Comments:

2. Was the information presented helpful to you?
   Yes _____
   No _____
   Somewhat _____
   Comments:

3. Was the presentation interesting?
   Yes _____
   No _____
   Somewhat _____
   Comments:

4. Was the presentation understandable?
   Yes _____
   No _____
   Somewhat _____
   Comments:

5. Did the speaker seem knowledgeable about the subject?
   Yes _____
   No _____
   Somewhat _____
   Comments:

6. Do you have suggestions for future speakers or topics?

Table 6.2   Evaluation of Group

Date _____

1. Did you feel comfortable in the group? If not, why not?
2. Was the group helpful to you?
3. What was most helpful to you?
4. What changes did you notice in yourself as a result of attending the group?
5. Did the group help you in the way you expected? If not, what had you expected to get from the group?
6. Are there other topics you would have liked to see addressed in the group?
7. Would you recommend the group to a friend?
8. Would you like more input from the leader?
9. Would you like more time for discussion?
10. If you left the group after a few sessions please explain why.
11. Add any comments.

Another assessment method asks each group member to reply to a mailed evaluation shortly after the termination of service. These should be sent to everyone who signs up for a group, even if they drop out after one or two sessions. There are reasons why those bereaved do not continue to attend. Their responses may provide important information on needs not met and approaches that are not effective.

CONCLUSION

Unstructured bereavement support groups are of tremendous value to the community and to the bereaved, who can attend as time and inclination dictate. They fill a need for those who are unaffiliated with any formal bereavement assistance program. The open and ongoing aspects of the group are appealing to many who do not want to commit or plan ahead. Unstructured, however, does not mean unplanned or unrehearsed. In spite of the lack of predictability of group size and tenor, the facilitators must be predictable by being present, professional, and prepared.

Chapter 7

Groups for Special Populations

Mixed bereavement support groups benefit participants because they learn that all loss engenders grief and that grief is a common human complaint (Slagle, 1983). They oftentimes feel heartened by the ways that others cope with grief, by the courage of someone whose grief seems worse than theirs, and by the example of grievers who are overcoming their grief and have made progress because of the passage of time and the work they have done to deal with their feelings of loss. Mixed groups are far better than no groups, which may be the only alternative in areas with small populations.

Groups geared to special populations have an advantage in that the group members experience the relief of finally being around others who, because of the similarity of their loss, seem really to understand. The bereaved can relax and feel free to say what they are feeling and thinking when they do not have to worry about horrifying anyone or being told that they should not think or feel the way they do. Because of the specific problems that one group of bereaved face but that others do not, they are better able to see examples and hear suggestions about how others have managed. It is more comfortable to be with people who are close enough to the problem that they do not need long explanations to achieve under-standing (Gorer, 1965).

There are many established national groups dedicated to helping survivors of certain kinds of deaths. They are volunteer groups with proven performances, which provide services to the bereaved at no charge.

Anyone wanting to start a group for a specific population of mourners should check with the reference librarian to obtain the addresses of these national organizations and profit from their demonstrated success and the authority of their names. They can supply guidance and materials. Because many of the groups are well known, new groups will achieve credibility through association with them. Most books that address bereavement have appendices that list all the organizations that provide bereavement services, including addresses and telephone numbers (Crenshaw, 1990). Look at these books for initial information, and get the most recent addresses and telephone numbers from the library. The group leaders can obtain helpful support and expertise from organizations that have literature on the bereavement problems of people of various ages suffering different kinds of losses.

WIDOWED PERSONS

Widowed persons in grief have special problems because of the major life-style changes they face. Their energy no longer goes toward the spouse. They have no one else to consider when making decisions. They feel adrift. These and other symptoms of grief need to be recognized when working with the widowed.

Widowed persons in different age groups have different priorities and needs. The young widowed have child-care and work concerns (Nudel, 1986). The middle-aged widowed have to revise their social lives and their plans for the future. The older widowed person has to gather resources to cope with a world that is unfamiliar after a lifetime of marriage.

There are organizations available to offer help and support to the widowed of all ages. Two groups are especially well organized and reach many of the widowed: Widowed Persons Service is a national organization that emphasizes one-to-one outreach. The many local chapters provide no-cost bereavement support services to all widowed people. Some of these local chapters have specialized groups for widowers and for the young widowed. *Theos,* the Greek word for God, is also an acronym for They Help Each Other Spiritually, a nationwide organization, with local chapters. It is supported through chapter charter fees and monthly monetary contributions from its members, who concentrate on support for young and middle-aged widowed and their families. Bereavement support groups are sponsored by the local chapters.

Additionally, many local funeral homes, churches, hospitals, and hospices sponsor ongoing and closed-end support groups for the widowed.

SUICIDE SURVIVORS

Survivors of suicide victims confront more guilt and more questions than many other groups of bereaved (O'Connor, 1984). Suicide is a shameful or disenfranchised death that intensifies the loneliness and despair of the survivors. Other people do not know what to say to them, and the mourners do not know how to explain what has happened. There may be real and justified anger at the deceased or severe conflict because of religious beliefs and values. The survivors may be so embarrassed by the suicide that they do not want to face others.

National agencies provide suicide prevention services; they help to explain suicide and offer support to friends and families of the suicide victims. None of them, however, provide grief support groups for suicide survivors. Some local groups have sprung up. They have found that relatives and friends of persons who commit suicide respond well to the support of others who are experiencing some of the same guilt, shame, and social censure that they feel.

SURVIVORS OF HOMICIDE VICTIMS

Homicide victims suffer untimely, often brutal deaths and leave survivors with intense anguish, anger, murderous feelings, and a sense of outrage and injustice (Jonas, 1983). They no longer see the world as a safe place. They are involved in the tracking, arresting, and, if the perpetrator is found, the prosecuting of the murderer. It is a long, painful, and frustrating ordeal that goes on for years.

Survivors of homicide victims need to know that they are not going crazy with rage. They need help to deal with the legal system. They can use advocacy services. They often find relief through working on something that can make a difference, such as the passage of a law or stricter sentencing and release standards. Through all of this they are pursued by the news media. The survivors are faced with being watchdogs for the department of corrections. They find they have to be ever vigilant in fighting parole, work-release, and early release for the murderers.

Siblings of a murdered family member are frequently urged to take care of their parents. They feel that their own distress over the loss is ignored (Schiff, 1986).

The parents of a murdered child have trouble maintaining their marriage because of their unhappiness, their different grief processes, and their inability to help each other. Parents need help to help their grieving children.

Parents of Murdered Children and Other Survivors of Homicide Victims is a national organization that sends out a newsletter, supports advocacy, provides literature, and sponsors local bereavement support groups for friends, parents, and siblings of murder victims. They encourage separate groups for siblings. The groups are ongoing and participants come and go as their need for support waxes and wanes.

DEATH BY DRUNKEN DRIVER

When friends and relatives are killed by drunken drivers, the survivors can suffer such rage that they fear for their own sanity. They experience intrusive thoughts and nightmares about car crashes. They may have strong feelings of wanting to seek vengeance and even feel that it is their duty to do so. Their grief experience becomes prolonged if the drunken driver survives and court proceedings take place. They, like homicide survivors, are often caught up in the grief and advocacy of the perpetrators' families. Seeing others take the part of the person who caused the death of their loved ones aggravates their volatile feelings.

Mothers Against Drunk Driving (MADD) is a national organization that fosters national awareness, is active in advocacy, provides literature, and sponsors bereavement support groups for friends and relatives of victims. They suggest either open-end or closed-end groups, with the closed-end groups following one after another. If numbers allow, they recommend separate groups for siblings, who can become overwhelmed with the parents' grief.

DEATH OF A CHILD

Grief is all encompassing when a child dies. The child made an impact and had value, regardless of age. When the child dies, even before birth, all hopes for the child's future and the knowledge of what the child might have been are lost (Chmurski, 1990). Relatives and friends are quick to reassure the parents that there will be more children or to say that at least they have other children. Because another child cannot take the place of the lost child, these statements further aggravate the distress. Problems result in families because everyone's grief is experienced in singular ways and in ways that other family members may not understand. They cannot fulfill each other's longings and cannot find support for their own distress. Families need help when a child dies, and organizations have been established to help.

Share is a nonprofit, nondenominational organization that provides literature, a newsletter, and support groups for parents who have lost children through miscarriage, stillbirth, or infant death. They supply educational material and telephone support and help set up bereavement support groups for parents.

The Compassionate Friends, Inc., a national organization, backs self-help support groups. Chapters are located throughout the country. By contacting the national office one can obtain a referral to a local chapter and a chapter contact person, information on bereavement, a resource guide, and a quarterly newsletter. Compassionate Friends groups are ongoing and open to anyone who has experienced the death of a child.

Literature and group sessions are also available to grandparents and siblings.

The National Sudden Infant Death Syndrome Foundation supports local chapters that are open to all parents who have suffered the death of a child through SIDS. The organization's self-help groups include a professional sponsor; they are ongoing, and parents can come and go as needed.

Besides these organized groups many funeral homes, hospices, and hospitals sponsor support groups for parents whose child has died.

COMMUNITY DISASTER

A community disaster is a devastating event that affects most of the people who live, work, or are otherwise involved in a particular locality (Walsh & Ruez, 1987). The community may be the country, state, or city. It may also be a school, workplace, club, team, or organization. When the disaster is a death it frequently involves not only the loss of the person but also devastation in the form of loss of income, home, or possessions.

Disastrous events that cause unexpected, untimely, and unacceptable death are horrifying to the people caught up in the episode (Kübler-Ross, 1974). Murders, suicides, destructive fires, natural disasters, and fatal crashes have deleterious effects on those who were threatened, who were embroiled in the events themselves, and those who assisted the victims and survivors of the catastrophe. Unless there is immediate bereavement support, those involved may suffer the consequences of a stressful trauma, which include physical symptoms such as stomachaches, headaches, and sleeping and eating problems, as well as feelings of guilt and rage, worry and insecurity, indecision and malaise, self-doubt and self-blame, and preoccupation with the event and with death. To counteract the emotional effects of a large-scale tragedy, the survivors need an opportunity to meet and talk about their experiences. Short-term bereavement support of one to three sessions, following a debriefing format, will provide immediate needed relief. The following model for such a support group session is based on the critical incident stress debriefing procedure (Critical Incident Stress Debriefers of Florida, Inc., 1989).

1   Meet with the survivors a day or two after the disaster in an area where they can be protected from interruptions, curiosity seekers, fact finders, and the news media.

2   Stress confidentiality.

3   Give the up-to-date facts of the situation. Has the murderer been apprehended? Did the suicide victim leave a note? Is the fire under control? How are the injured doing? What specific action has been taken?

4   Assure the group that no one has to talk if they do not want to.

5   Go around the circle asking each participant what happened to him or her. What did they see? What did they do?

6   Address the group one by one; what did each one think at the time of the disaster?

7   Another time around the circle, the participants are encouraged to share their reactions. What was the worst that happened?

8   Ask those present to share their symptoms if they want to.

9   Next reassure the group participants that their reactions, feelings, and thoughts are normal. They are under severe stress. How have they handled stress in the past? How have they handled their present distress? The leader suggests ways to cope.

10   The facilitator asks for further questions or comments.

11   Helpful resources are offered.

12   If appropriate, another meeting is scheduled.

The facilitator in such a group does not correct any speaker, does not ask clarifying questions, or urge the participants to express themselves more fully or in alternate ways. The point of the conclave is to allow the survivors the opportunity to hear the latest information, to hear what others saw and felt, to learn that their reactions are normal and acceptable, to be prepared for the symptoms of stress, to learn some coping skills, and to know that help is available if they want or need it.

This type of support is given in response to a critical incident and is limited to one to three sessions. If the desire exists for more support, the survivors are made aware of other resources in the community.

CHILDREN EXPERIENCING THE LOSS OF A LOVED ONE

Children at different ages have different needs and different understandings of death; they require help that is appropriate to their developmental ages. Children under seven, and sometimes until nine, do not understand that dead is dead and the person is gone forever (Kastenbaum, 1967). Their security is their parents. They feel guilty and often think they are to blame if someone close to them dies. They think in concrete terms and want to know how someone who is dead functions. They ask questions that have to do with sleeping, eating, and bodily functions to try to figure out how the dead "manage."

As children grow older they have a better understanding that dead is for all time, but they still tend to feel guilty and worry that they may have done something that contributed to the person's death. They are uncomfortable if their situation is too different from other children's situations and may lie about a death in the family, denying that it occurred. Peers and acceptance are important to them. They may talk with their friends when they will not talk to family members, or they may refuse to talk with anyone.

Children grieve in short bursts. They grieve a loss at various times over the years, as their development and understanding change. They do not sustain grief for a prolonged period, but they will grieve at intervals for a long time, as their comprehension matures. Grief can be expressed in many ways. Depression, anger, acting out, delinquent behavior, poor scholarship, dependency, difficulties in relationships, phobias, regression, inability to sleep or loss of appetite, fears, physical problems, overidentification with the dead person, and suicidal thoughts or actions are all symptoms of grief in children (Van Ornum & Mordock, 1990).

Rainbows is an international sponsor of support groups for children in grief led by professionals trained for three to six hours in the Rainbows approach. The sessions are held in churches, schools, or anyplace children congregate. There is a set program for each age group. The meetings are 30 to 40 minutes long and are held once a week for 12 weeks. Children who have experienced loss through divorce and through death attend groups together.

The Compassionate Friends, Inc., sometimes sponsors groups for siblings of children who have died. In some localities Widowed Persons Service has groups for children whose father or mother has died. Hospices often provide art therapy, play groups, or talk groups for children in grief. Many schools schedule groups on campus for students who are dealing with the loss of a loved one. These groups may be open- or closed-end; they can also be short-term groups established in response to a tragedy that has affected the community or because of the death of a teacher or student. Groups may be small or large depending on the approach and the problem that is being addressed. When an assembly is called so that children can meet to obtain information or ask questions about a community or student body calamity, the group will be very large. This curtails rumors but does not always meet the needs of individual children. When this technique is used, it is crucial for teachers and counselors to meet later with small groups of children. If children are to feel comfortable and have the opportunity for individual expression, there should be no more than 5 to 10 children in a group.

Children's Grief Groups

Death is devastating to children in the present and affects them into the future. Grief groups for children help, but good planning is essential (Haasl & Marnocha, 1990). Because of developmental differences, many leaders of children's grief groups divide the participants by age. Other leaders have success with children of all ages in one group. Some limit groups to school-age children. There are groups offered just for preschool-age children, but the ability to verbalize, share, attend, and manage some self-care are essential to the group process.

Coleaders—both of whom should be trained in group work and working with children—are recommended. Two are better than one because they will have to cope with acting-out children, assist younger children, set up materials for activities, and fill in for each other when one leader is out because of vacation or sick leave. It is always effective, too, to have a person available to devote time to first-time participants in an established group.

Bereavement support groups for children take a great deal of energy. This is another reason to have coleaders and a reason to limit the sessions to one hour (Fitzgerald, 1993). Also, children tire and their attention spans are short. If the group is held at the end of the school day, the children have already been active for many hours. Some facilitators hold the group for one and one-half hours but allow time at the end for snacking and socializing.

The room chosen for the meetings should be cheerful, private (the group's own room), and set up for wear and tear. It has to be a room where children can talk freely, yell, and engage in physical activity without feeling as though they are doing the wrong thing.

Some groups meet twice a week, some weekly, and some monthly. All of these schedules are effective. The arrangement depends on the children and the availability, preferences, and energies of the leaders.

Involve parents. Although the parents do not attend the sessions with the children, one or two sessions should be scheduled just for them. Before the beginning date of the children's group, and when children join an ongoing group, the purpose and process of the group can be explained. After the group has been meeting for a while, the children and parents meet with the facilitators again. The children display pictures they have drawn and explain how the drawings depict their feelings and experiences (Nelson, 1989). At the end of a series of sessions, or after the children have attended for a period of time in an ongoing group, a meeting with parents can be held to help them better cope with their children, to help them understand what the children have learned, and to coach them on how they can give their children further assistance and support (National Institute of Mental Health, 1979). In the interim, the leaders will want to brief the parents and respond to their concerns and questions (Fitzgerald, 1992). This is another good reason for having cofacilitators.

Handouts are useful tools because the parents can refer to them when they run into problems. Suggestions for handouts appear in Table 7.1.

Children go to grief groups to learn, to be heard, and have their feelings understood and accepted. The children learn from one another, share with one another, and help one another. As in adult groups, the leaders set the structure and the agenda. Also as in adult groups, the participants learn that they can help others. The facilitators help the children develop the tools to make the group a self-help group.

Table 7.1 Handout for Parents

Talking with Children in Grief

1. Be direct. Use the correct words. Say "dead." Do not use words that soft-pedal what happened. Children are not able to generalize from the words "sleeping," "gone," or "lost." They will believe that the person is lost, sleeping, or gone for a while, all of which imply that the person will come back.

2. Do not go into detail or give long explanations. Give the facts. Wait for questions. Answer the questions. If you do not know the answer, do not guess or make something up. Admit that you do not know. If you can find out the answer from another source, tell the child that, and follow through.

3. Find out what the children are thinking. Ask the children what they have heard and what they think has happened.

4. Talk about your feelings. If you look sad or are crying, explain why. Let children know that the unhappy feelings are in no way related to them, but that you are mourning the death of the loved one.

5. Reassure the children that they will be cared and provided for.

6. Talk about the person who died. Bring up fond memories and other memories too.

7. Talk about the procedures that surround the death, such as the wake, funeral, memorial service, cremation, burial, and visitation. Explain what will happen and give the child an opportunity to participate.

8. Read a children's book about death to the child.

9. Praise children when they are functioning well so they will feel more able and not so out-of-control. However, do not ask them to be grown up and take on adult responsibilities and behaviors.

10. A hug is always nice.

11. Make sure the children know what caused the death and that it is not related to anything they did, is not a punishment, and is not contagious. They will not catch it and neither will you. Assure them that you will be around for a long time.

12. Be prepared to repeat explanations and give the information again and again.

Helping Children Through Grief

1. Return to the normal household schedule as quickly as possible. Children feel more secure with their regular routine.

2. Let the children know that they are protected and safe. When they feel secure, they will be able to live through their grief.

3. Try to understand the children's behavior. If they do not have the words, they will express their grief through their behavior.

4. Involve the children in a ceremony that gives them an opportunity to say good-bye to their loved one.

5. Talk about bad dreams, or have the children draw a picture of the dream. Have them rip up the picture and throw it away. This gets rid of the dreams.

6. Do not be alarmed if the children play at dying or death. This is a way for them to work through their feelings and fears.

7. It is meaningful for the child to do something to memorialize the loved one.

8. Plan something for the child to look forward to, such as a vacation or other enjoyable experience.

9. Let the children help out in age-appropriate ways.

10. When you are not available, make sure the children know that someone trustworthy is present.

11. Look at pictures of the deceased together.

12. Give the children tangible mementos of the person who died.

13. Let children stay children. Do not lean on them for comfort and support.

14. Let the school know of the death, and let the children know you are doing this. They may not want you to. Do it anyway. It is better for the children to know that the teacher and the other children know about the death, than to suspect that they *might* know.

The objectives of a children's grief group are

1   To provide a safe and caring place for children to learn about death.
2   To help children understand that all feelings are OK.
3   To teach children how to experience and express feelings.
4   To give children the opportunity to meet others who are going through grief and engage in mutual help.
5   To assist children to look to their futures with confidence and pleasant anticipation.
6   To encourage the recall and sharing of good memories.
7   To understand the importance of the deceased in their lives.

Children appreciate predictability. Group sessions that stick to a routine are comfortable for them. They know what to do and what happens next. They have had enough disruption in their lives. If new participants join an ongoing group, the old hands take pleasure in introducing the recruit to the schedule. This gives them importance and a feeling of being in control. A suggested agenda is as follows:

1. Set up and ongoing projects.   The children are not likely to arrive all at one time. The early ones can get out supplies and busy themselves with the regular routine and ongoing projects until everyone arrives. Children new to the group can be given individual attention by one of the leaders or be introduced to the procedures by the children. Some ongoing activities might be the following:

- The children place a star after their names to mark their attendance.
- They draw pictures of, or write out, one happy and one unhappy experience and post them on the "What Happened to You This Week?" boards.
- They select their mood color and pin it on themselves. (The first group session will not run like this, as the children have to be oriented to the expectations and procedures. They will learn that different colors stand for different moods and will pick the color that most depicts their mood when they arrive for the day.)
- The children may have started projects in the previous session that they want to complete.
- The participants will add to the ongoing collage, which can be made from pictures cut from magazines or by freehand drawing. The collage theme can be the funeral, life at home, favorite memories, or anything the children suggest.

2. Opening and closing song or group recitation.   The song or recitation can be anything that is short, peppy, and cheerful. "Hail, Hail, the Gang's All Here" is fine. This ritual develops a sense of belonging.

3. *Sharing time.* This can occur at the beginning or the end of the session. Because children are eager to tell what they want to tell, encouraging sharing in the beginning keeps them from being distracted by their thoughts for the rest of the hour. Everyone has the opportunity to share. Nothing is too silly. No one makes fun of anyone. It is at this time that the rules of the group are made known, reiterated for each new group member, and brought out as reminders when necessary. Some suggested rules:

- Confidentiality. They may tell others about what they say and do in the group but are not to tell what anyone else in the group says or does.
- One person speaks at a time.
- No one has to speak if they do not want to.
- No one makes fun of what another person says or does.

4. *Group activity.* *Introductions.* The first group activity is introductions. Children state their names, ages, who died, and what caused the death. This is done each time a new member joins the group. Children are curious. They will want to know. They may ask questions.

Mementos are wonderful. They are important to children. Ask them to bring in pictures, items, or tapes to share with the group.

Ask the children to circulate and find something about another child that is like them. It could be the color of their eyes, age, where they attend school, or a favorite food. This gets the children interacting and also lets them know that they all have some things in common.

Instruct each child to share his or her favorite memory of the person who died. They may also share an unhappy memory.

Help the children make a "reporter-on-the-street" video. They can interview each other about their lives and about the group. They may want to show it to their families.

Write a story about a death. Involve all the children. One of the facilitators writes, while the children suggest ideas about who is in the story, what happens to them, and how it all turns out. Press for a happy ending.

Draw a tree without leaves. Ask the children to put leaves on the tree. Every leaf is someone they can count on. They are displaying their support system. After they have identified their immediate family, ask about neighbors, teachers, church people, friends, the doctor, and any other professional people they see. Urge them to look far and wide for people who are involved in their lives.

Guided imagery can create a moving experience for children. Have them close their eyes while the facilitator takes them for an imaginary walk in a lovely garden where they meet the person who died. Their loved one gives them a gift. What is the gift? Talk about it afterwards.

Draw a pepperoni pizza or the ripples that a pebble makes when it is thrown into the water. This symbolically shows how the grief subsides as the pepperoni is eaten or as the ripples make less and less impression as they get farther from where the pebble hit the water. Ask the children where they are in their grief.

Talk about death and loss. Children name other losses they have experienced. They have lost toys, teeth—what else? Pets have died. Did other people die? How did they feel when there were losses? How long did they feel that way?

A feeling game gives the children an opportunity to list all the feelings they know, to act out a feeling and have the other participants guess what it is, and then talk about times when that feeling occurs. Include positive and negative feelings.

Teach the children progressive relaxation. This gives them a tool to use when they get upset. Have them suggest appropriate times to put this skill to work.

Ask the children to name both negative and positive feelings, starting with the feelings that they are having right now. List the feelings. Ask them to give the feelings colors, such as

    red-angry
    blue-peaceful
    black-sad
    green-jealous
    yellow-happy
    orange-excited
    brown-afraid
    purple-worried
    pink-content
    white-neutral
    gray-mean

The children can come up with the colors, the feelings that correspond to the colors, and reasons why certain colors represent particular feelings.

The children can write and act a play about a death.

Devise a word game in which unfamiliar and familiar words are used that deal with death. This will help them learn the meaning of words such as *casket, urn,* and *mortician.* The game could be fitting words with pictures, a trivia game, or a board game.

Break a clay pot. Give each child a piece. On each piece the child writes an unhappy emotion. Then they rebuild the pot, gluing it back together. This symbolizes the disruption caused by death and getting their lives back in order. Because children think symbolically, this is an effective exercise that helps them conceptualize.

Read a story about death, letting the children fill in the blanks. They will identify the important characters and decide on the important turns the story takes.

A group collage with three parts—how they felt before the death occurred, how they felt after the death, and how they feel now—will have all of the children working together.

Bring in a bag and ask the children to fill it with their feelings of anger. As each one tells about something that makes them angry, put an object into the bag. Soon it will be too big to carry around. How can they unload some of that anger so that the bag is not huge and overwhelming? Suggest ways to solve problems and manage anger. The children will have ideas too.

Play "To Tell the Truth." Devise questions or sentence-completion topics, one to a slip of paper. The children will draw a slip and respond, telling the truth. Examples of the type of statements to be used are, I wonder if _____; I wish _____; If only _____; I could _____; I am angry about _____. There can also be questions: What is hardest for you to do? What would you like to tell the person who died? What would make it easier for you? What advice do you have for your family? What is the funniest thing you remember about the person who died?

Ask questions and have the children brainstorm the answers. They can get silly if they like. They will still learn. Some of the questions to use are, What can you do instead of hitting? What helps when you are angry? What are some ways to make yourself happy?

When the children know each other better, put out envelopes, one for each child, with the child's name written on it. Everyone in the group is to write one nice thing about everybody else in the room and put one slip in each person's envelope.

Write the word Love on the board. Ask the children what love is, how people show love, whom they love, and how people let them know that they are loved.

5. Individual activity. *The children are instructed to write a letter to the deceased saying anything and everything they think and feel.* If they do not have writing skills, they can draw a picture for their loved one.

Children draw their own coat of arms. It is divided into six parts.

A special memory

A picture that displays their favorite things

What they will be doing ten years from now

A picture that shows something that everyone in their family would like

Something that the deceased liked

Something that the family did together

Ask the children to do a profile of themselves by writing down all of their favorite things: their favorite color, food, song, holiday, season, sport, movie, television program, actor, actress, teacher, friend, article of clothing, book, car, game, flower, state, animal, game, restaurant.

Have the children focus on themselves by writing out their age, hair and eye color, height and weight, and what they like best about themselves. What do they think others like best about them?

Assign the children the task of drawing five faces, all showing a different feeling. Under each face write when they had that emotion.

Draw a grid. The children write one letter of their name in each square of the grid. Then they write feelings using each of the letters as the first letter of the word (see Figure 7.1). Ask the children when they had any of these feelings. Which feelings were hard for them?

Building something out of clay. Talk about it. They may smash the clay object if they want to.

Write the dead person's name on the outside of a helium-filled balloon. Take the balloon outside and let it go free.

Request that the children draw a picture of something that is hard for them to do since the death, what they miss the most, or what they wish they could do over. They can then talk about their pictures.

Write the children's fears on balloons. Let the children pop them.

The children can be given pictures, objects, and materials for drawing so that they can accumulate a good feelings box. When something makes them feel good, they may add an item to those already in their box.

Figure 7.1   Sample Name and Feelings Grid

Give the children a supply of white paper plates. On each plate they can draw a picture showing how their individual family members act or look when they are feeling sad or glad.

Direct the children to draw a picture of their families before and after the death. Show them doing a favorite family activity (Fitzgerald, 1993; Haasl & Marnocha, 1990).

6. *Closing song or recitation.* It can be the same one used during the opening ritual, or a different one.

7. *Refreshments.* Ending each session with a treat is nice. Try to avoid foods with high sugar content so that the children will not become hyperactive, or messy foods that are sticky and hard to clean up.

All of the exercises contribute to achieving the objectives of the children's bereavement support group. They are designed to help the children feel safe and cared for, to help them learn about death, and to experience and express feelings. The children learn to help each other, to look forward to their future, to recall favorite memories, and to respect the importance of the deceased in their lives.

Structured, closed-end bereavement support groups for children can be devised so that children of different ages can meet in the same group. It works well if some of the older children can assist the facilitator with the younger children. This is a therapeutic technique because it gives the children a role. The children who are doing the helping are able to make a contribution and see themselves as fulfilling an important function. The children who are being helped learn that there are many people in their environment who are interested in them and many people who can provide succor. All of them learn compassion as they become attached to each other and recognize the sorrow that each of them is feeling. Younger children appreciate the older children's grief and feel less alone. The older children are impressed with the pluck of the younger ones, recognizing that life is unfair to others as well.

Groups segregated by age are easier on the facilitators and the children. Children at about the same level of understanding have similar interests. There is a shorter adjustment period, and they are not put off at the prospect of having to attend a group with children whose age range is not compatible with their own. When the sessions are not geared to one age group, planning is more difficult.

Older children can do more talking therapy, whereas sessions for the younger ones need to be more activity oriented. Groups for younger children need a higher staff-participant ratio because they require more supervision. Materials must be watched more closely. Equipment cannot be left lying around when it is not in use because it may be destroyed by children too young to know how to take care of it. The children must also be kept safe from hurting themselves with toxic substances or articles small enough to swallow or stick in an ear.

The following is an example of a structured bereavement support group for elementary-school-age children. It must be emphasized that the sessions outlined are examples. Every age, every group, and all facilitators will require different activities and approaches. The facilitators have to feel comfortable with the material to make it work for the children. The sample agenda will have to be reworked by the facilitators to fit their style.

SESSION ONE-GETTING TO KNOW ONE ANOTHER

Topics

1 Getting acquainted.
2 Why we are here.

Objectives

1 The participants will be able to talk about the death of their loved ones.
2 The participants will understand that everybody grieves when a loved one dies.

Materials Needed

1 Flip chart and magic markers.
2 Paper, glue, and magazines to cut up.
3 Paper and colored markers for all the children to use.

Activities

The facilitators introduce themselves and greet the children, explaining that they will be together for X number of sessions and meet X times a week, that everyone here has experienced the death of a loved one and feels sad, but that they will work together to help themselves and each other understand what happened, figure out ways to handle it, and feel better.

Introductions and Sharing Time   The children are asked to introduce themselves and mark themselves present on the prepared chart that will remain in the room and be ready for them at each session. Have colored pens or stickers that not only indicate their presence, but their mood. As the children introduce themselves and go to mark themselves present, ask them to indicate their mood with the designated color or stickers. Have the stickers or the colors that indicate the mood labeled so they do not have to remember the formula. At first, start with few mood variations, such as sad or glad, afraid, worried, or excited. More moods and colors can be added as time goes on, but at the first session it should not be too complicated.

The introductions include name, age, where they go to school, and who died. The sooner the ice is broken about the reason for the meeting, the better. Curiosity and anxiety are satisfied, and everyone can get about the real reason for the group. Soft-pedaling or skirting the issue increases anxiety.

Share the rules of the group:

- Confidentiality. No one is to repeat what someone else says in the group. They may tell what they say, but everything else is confidential.
- One person speaks at a time; no one has to speak if they do not want to.
- No one makes fun of what another person says or does.

Group Activity   Initiate a group activity. The beginning group activity should be an ongoing one that the children can work on if they come early to a session, when they have completed a project, or if they stay late. A collage about the death, starting when they first heard about it and continuing to the present, is good. They will be able to include pictures that represent feelings, people, and activities. They can draw pictures or cut them out of magazines. The collage needs to be hung or laid out in an area where they may go to work on it as time and inclination permit.

Individual Activity   Pass out a sheet and ask the children to write down the names of all the people involved in their daily lives. Identify them by roles, so the children will be prompted to think of them. If they do not know names, they can write descriptions. The categories of people are parents, grandparents, siblings, neighbors, aunts, uncles, cousins, friends, teachers, clergy, postal carriers, store clerks, babysitters, barber, dentist, doctor, beautician, coaches, and so on. Do not set up a competition to see who can make the longest list. Ask the children to write what they like about each person on the list. Be excited about the number of people involved in their lives. Make sure that they all understand that although they have experienced an important loss, they have not lost everyone. There are others who care and who are helpful. Keep their papers for discussion during the next session.

Group Song   Introduce the idea of a group song. The children may suggest one, or the leaders may have some to suggest. Anything is OK, as long as it is short and peppy. Perhaps they will come up with two songs. One can be sung at the beginning of the meeting, and the other at the end.

Refreshments   There are several approaches possible in regard to the refreshments. The children can take turns bringing something, there can be a new delight each session, or the menu can be set, with the same snacks served each time. Each has advantages and disadvantages. The children receive enjoyment and recognition for providing treats for the others, and there is the symbolic gesture of being in control to the extent that they can do something for someone else. However, doing this may place too much stress on an already stressed household; because of the disruption in their lives they may forget, or there may be financial pressures that make providing treats difficult. It also may be taken personally if the children do not like what they bring. If the facilitators plan the menu, and different treats are selected for each session, the children have the excitement of a surprise. Doing this, however, puts a strain on the facilitators, who always have to come up with something different that is appetizing and meets the standards of being easy to serve and easy to clean up. There is comfort in a set menu in that it is predictable and children in grief need to have as much predictability in their lives as possible. Perhaps the best choice is a compromise, with a few alternative selections, so that all palates can be satisfied but the facilitators are not challenged to come up with something new each time the group gets together.

SESSION TWO-WHO CAN HELP AND HOW WE FEEL

Topics

1   Who can help.
2   Feelings.

Objectives

1   The participants will recognize that there are many helpful people in their lives.
2   The participants will recognize and accept their feelings.

Materials Needed

1   Flip chart and magic markers.
2   Paper, glue, and magazines to cut up.
3   Paper and colored markers for all the children to use.
4   Vignettes that describe feelings or pictures of people experiencing different emotions.

Activities

Set up and Ongoing Projects   Greet all arrivals. Ask the early arrivals to help set out the materials, or direct them to the ongoing collage project. Have everyone who comes in mark themselves present, selecting a sticker or marker to indicate their mood. Add a couple more feelings to the mood chart, such as "peaceful" and "jealous." Point out these additions to the children.

Group Song   When it is time to begin the meeting, start singing the group song.

Sharing Time   Ask the children to introduce themselves again, adding another fact about themselves, such as what they like to do for fun.

After all the introductions ask the children to tell about something that happened at their house since the last session. The facilitators should try to ask at least one question to elicit another fact, or in the context of this session, a feeling. If the story a child recounted was about someone else, ask how that person felt. If it is about them, ask how they felt.

Group Activity   Follow up on the individual exercise of the last session. Return the children's worksheets to them, and ask them to report the categories of people who are active in their lives. As they volunteer information, write the categories on the flip chart. There should be neighbors, professional people, business people, and many others, including the facilitators. Make sure they understand that although they lost important people, they still have many important people in their lives. Use this activity as a bridge to talking in greater depth about feelings and their grief.

Start the discussion of feelings by talking about their moods of the day and why they think they feel as they do. Make the feelings as normal and universal as possible by identifying other children who feel the same way today or have felt that way.

Continue the discussion of feelings by telling short stories about children in different situations, and ask them how they think that child felt. The stories should be about a child who experienced the death of a loved one, a child who missed school and failed a test, a child whose friend found another friend and did not include him or her, a child who got what he or she wanted for Christmas, a child who did a courageous or kind deed, a child who was selected to make a speech in a school program, or a child who hit a home run or managed some other achievement. Write these and all the feelings mentioned on the flip chart.

Now show pictures of people in different situations and pictures of faces expressing emotions. Ask the children what they think the person or people feel and what is going on that causes them to feel that way. Write these feelings on the flip chart too.

Show acceptance, understanding, and approval of all feelings. Show that people can have both sad and glad feelings. Weave into the vignettes examples of people who were hurt, disappointed, lost a loved one, and then had a happy experience, to demonstrate that no mood is permanent and no pain lasts forever. The facilitators may want to share anecdotes from their own lives or the lives of others that illustrate the principle of sunshine following the rain.

Individual Activity   Give the children printed sheets that ask them to list their favorite food, game, sport, teacher, animal, song, television program, flower, actor or actress, book, car, song, or anything the facilitators want to include. This is to give the children the idea that their lives are multidimensional, so include as many categories as possible. Besides demonstrating the many outlets and interests in their lives, this exercise conveys the concept that one very sad loss does not mean that all is lost. Collect the papers and save them for the next meeting, when the principle of this project can be pointed out.

It is good if the children can discover this and other principles on their own, but do not expect them to make the connections without help. Coach and guide them. If necessary, tell them.

Closing Song

Refreshments

SESSION THREE-WHO WE ARE AND WHAT WE REMEMBER

Topics

1 Everybody is special.
2 Memories.

Objectives

1 The participants will recognize that they are like others and different from others.
2 The participants will identify fond memories of their loved ones.

Materials Needed

1 Flip chart and magic marker.
2 Paper, glue, and magazine to cut up.
3 Paper and colored markers for all the children to use.
4 Tape recorder and a cassette for each child.

Activities

Set up and Ongoing Projects   Greet all arrivals and go through the routine of soliciting their help, encouraging them to work on the ongoing project, and having them mark themselves present and indicate their mood. Add a couple more feelings, such as "angry" and "content."

Group Song   Get the group going with the group song.

Sharing Time   The children are to introduce themselves again, including one more fact, such as who else lives in their households.
It is their time to share. They are encouraged to talk about happy and unhappy events and tell what happened in their lives since the last session. As before, use examples from their stories to teach them about feelings and behaviors and that they are not the only ones in their households who miss the deceased.

Group Activity   Return the children's papers from the last session. They are to circulate and find two other people who like two of the same favorites that they have on their list. They are also to find out if they have one favorite thing that no one else in the group has. Children who experience the death of a family member often feel set apart and different.

Finding people who share their preferences will help them feel more in tune with others.

At the same time, help them appreciate the ways in which they are unique. Discuss loss as a group exercise. Ask all of them if they ever knew anyone else who died. List the relationships on the flip chart. Did they have pets that died? Did they ever lose something that was important to them, such as a toy, their homework, a possession? Did they lose teeth or have their appendix or tonsils removed? Did they move and lose their old neighborhood and friends? Through all this, what did they gain? Did they make new friends, get a new house, grow new teeth? Help them understand that although loss is hard, there are many losses, and even though we do not want to lose what belongs to us, we also have gains.

Individual Activity   There is something about their loved ones that the children most want to remember; there may be several things. Ask them to think about this, make a list, write out an experience or incident. Is it something they did together? Something the loved one did for them or gave them? Was it something traditional? Give the children some examples. The facilitators can tell about a loss in their lives or the lives of people they know and about particular memories or memorabilia that are cherished. Give an instance of a happy memory.

Because the memories are important, work with one child at a time, and have him or her tell about the memory and record it on the cassette, which is given to the child to keep. Bring the recorder and cassettes to all future sessions so the children can add memories as they think of them.

Closing Song

Refreshments

A note to facilitators: By now it is apparent that these sessions are of simplified design. This is done to help facilitators who are not particularly artistic, or adept at crafts, or do not have access to many materials see the possibilities of a children's grief group that does not require elaborate exercises and a plethora of materials.

SESSION FOUR-WHO DIES AND HOW THEY DIE

Topics

1 Causes of death.
2 Questions about death.

Objectives

1 The participants will learn that there are many causes of death.
2 The participants will have their questions about death discussed.

Materials Needed

1 Flip chart and magic markers.
2 Paper, glue, and magazines to cut up.
3 Paper and colored markers for all the children to use.
4 Pictures of funerals and the paraphernalia that goes with them.

Activities

Set up and Ongoing Projects Go through the beginning routine of preparing the materials, involving the early arrivals, and marking attendance. Add two more feelings, such as "mean" or "disappointed," for the children to choose from.

Group Song If any of the participants want to lead the group in their song, let them do so.

Sharing Time Introduction time again. This time ask the children to include one positive thing about themselves. The facilitators can serve as models and examples can be given. They might like to report on an ability, something about their looks, or an aspect of their personality or character.

What has happened to them since the last session? Help them identify their feelings. Was the experience helpful or unhelpful? The focus on whether it was helpful or unhelpful to them or others is more supportive and constructive than whether it was right or wrong, good or bad.

Group Activity As a group, discuss how their loved ones died. Was it from sickness, accident, or murder? Ask each child to talk about the death. Make sure every one of them understands what actually happened. What do they think cancer is? Do they feel they had any responsibility in the person's death? What caused the death? If a story sounds unbelievable, check on the facts before making corrections. Some people do die in unbelievable circumstances.

Talk about the funeral. Who was there? How did people act? Find out whether they know the meaning of many of the words such as *coffin, mortuary, cremains.* What happened that they did not understand? If the facilitators can gather pictures of places and objects involved in death rituals, it would be helpful to display them. The pictures might be of cemeteries, urns, caskets, undertakers, hearses, or crypts. Children aged 9 to 12 are very curious, even fascinated, by the rituals of death.

Individual Activity   Ask each child to draw a picture of their loved one's sickness or funeral. Externalizing the feelings, fears, and facts through talking about them and drawing them helps free the children from them and will prevent or stop nightmares. Explain this to them. If any of the children are having nightmares, instruct them to draw a picture about it. To dramatize being rid of the nightmare, they can crush or tear the paper.

Ask each child to bring pictures of the loved one or memorabilia to the next session. Send a note home with them explaining what is appropriate. Do this before the last session so that if some of the children forget, they will not miss out on the exercise. If they forget and there is still one session left, they can bring in their memorabilia the next time.

Closing Song

Refreshments

SESSION FIVE-WHAT WE MISS AND HOW WE CAN HELP

Topics

1 Saying good-bye.
2 Helping others in grief.

Objectives

1 The participants will formulate what they miss and what they do not miss.
2 The participants will identify what helps them and others feel better.

Materials Needed

1 Flip chart and magic markers.
2 Paper, glue, and magazines to cut up.
3 Paper and colored markers for all the children to use.
4 Prepared slips that suggest ways to feel better. The ways might include talking to a friend, playing a board game or an athletic game, such as basketball or baseball, crying, looking at pictures, bike riding, reading, writing, helping someone else, talking to a parent, getting a hug, or getting a good grade.

Activities

Set up and Ongoing Projects   The children may have completed their collage by this time. Start them on another one that depicts all the things they like to do. Add two more feelings to the mood list, such as "upset" and "jolly."

Group Song

Sharing Time   As the children introduce themselves, ask them to include something they would like the others to know about themselves. If they seem stuck, suggest that they include their favorite thing that they ever did, what they like to do best, what subject they like in school, what they like about their best friend, what they got for their birthday, or anything the facilitators think would be meaningful, based on their observations of the children while they have been together.

What have they done since the last session that they would like to report to the group? Encourage them to find a happy event to report.

Use the sharing time for telling about the memorabilia and pictures they brought from home. Ask each child to display the pictures or the objects, explain what they are and why they are meaningful, and respond to questions from the other children. If it is possible to take a group picture of the children with their memorabilia, or separate pictures of each child, do so, and have them developed for distribution at the next session.

Group Activity   Engage the children in a discussion about what they miss the most since their loved one died. List these on the flip chart. Ask them to think also about what they do not miss. List those things too.

Ask the children what they do to feel better when they feel sad or when they think about the death of their loved one and are unhappy. It may not be necessary to use the prepared slips with the suggestions (see entry 4 in the materials needed section), but have them ready just in case. What have other people done for them that makes them feel better or more hopeful? What have they done, or what do they think they can do, to help other family members when they are sad? Make a list of everything they mention, and have copies ready to distribute to them at the next session.

Individual Activity   Ask each child to write a letter to the deceased, including all the things they want to tell them and bringing them up to date about their lives. They may keep this letter private or share it with the group members or with their family members.

Closing Song

Refreshments   Announce to the children that their family members are invited to join the group for refreshments during the last session.

A note to facilitators: If any of the children seem especially troubled, the facilitators should alert the child that they are going to talk to their parents or the people responsible for them so that they can get further help to get them through this unhappy time. In any case, the parents or guardians will need information about how the child did in the group and whether there are problems that they should know about. Having worked with the children, the facilitators can provide valuable information about the children's concerns and worries and suggest ways in which the family members can help them.

SESSION SIX-REMEMBERING AND SAYING GOOD-BYE

Topics

1 A remembrance.
2 What was learned.

Objectives

1 The participants will honor the deceased.
2 The participants will recognize what they learned.

Materials Needed

1 Flip chart and magic markers.
2 Paper, glue, and magazines to cut up.
3 Paper and colored markers for all the children to use.
4 Candles or appropriate materials for a short memorial service.

Activities

Set up and Ongoing Projects   Work continues on the collage of happy and enjoyable things to do. The facilitators will want to decide what to do with the two collages after the parents have seen them. Do they stay with the facilitators? Are they cut up and divided among the children? Do the children draw straws to see who gets them?

The children mark their attendance. Two more moods are added, such as "serious" and "sincere."

Group Song

Sharing Time   This time the children introduce each other and tell one nice thing about the person they introduce.

They may report on what they did in the interval since the last session, but also ask them to tell what they are looking forward to doing. Children need something to look forward to in times of sorrow. Press them to come up with something.

Group Activity   Suggest that the children have a memorial service to honor their loved ones. It can be as simple as drawing pictures of what they would like to give to the deceased and depositing these in a basket or appropriate receptacle, lighting candles, saying the name of the deceased, and blowing out the candles. This is a simple, but serious, moment and a meaningful ritual.

Individual Activity   Every child is assigned the task of writing one nice thing about every other person in the group and putting it in an envelope labeled with that person's name.

Their second individual task is to write at least two things that they learned in the group or two ways that the group helped them and leave these for the facilitators.

Closing Song

Refreshments   Because family members will be present, plan to make a little speech about how wonderful the children were, how hard they worked, and how much they will be missed.

CONCLUSION

Because there is national support and avid advocacy by many of the individuals who have experienced traumatic losses, there is backing for professionals and the bereaved who want to sponsor support groups for special populations. The projects are not only worthwhile, but richly rewarding. In many instances, help and guidance are available upon request. When it is up to the local facilitators to get the group off the ground, the suggestions in this chapter will provide direction.

Chapter 8

Group Participation Troubleshooting

If the bereavement support group does not offer what new participants want, they will screen themselves out and look elsewhere for the help they seek. On occasion, however, participants will try to subvert the group to their desires. This frustrates facilitators and group members. Unless the group can be returned to its original path and objectives, it will unravel. The participants who wanted something different will not achieve their goals, and the group members who were benefitting from the group will fall away. To avert disappointment and disillusionment, the facilitator will have to take preventive action. If the group has been in operation long enough for the group members to have coalesced, they will assist. In short-term, closed-end groups, however, and in open-end groups with a changing population, this is not likely to occur. What will happen is that the regular participants will be unhappy. They will grumble to each other, complain to the facilitator, or withdraw from the group. The facilitators will have to handle the problem.

PARTICIPANTS WHO NEED MORE THAN GROUP SUPPORT

There are bereavement group participants who need more than group support, but who can still attend group meetings, get additional help elsewhere, and profit from the various sources of assistance. There are, however, prospective participants who do not fit into the bereavement support group process. It is not good for them, and it is upsetting to the other group members. Some may do well with individual help. Some may do well in therapy groups set up to help clients with mental health problems. Some people, unfortunately, are chronically impaired and are unable to benefit from either individual or group help. As sad as this is, the group does not have to be sacrificed to their unanswered needs.

Participants who need individual help, and can also manage in a support group, are those with adjustment disorders and depressed and anxious moods. Family, financial, and social problems are all common in bereavement support groups, and are usually problems that were present long before the participants became bereaved. None of these difficulties necessarily precludes attending a bereavement support group.

Support groups cannot, however, incorporate individuals who are psychotic, suicidal, homicidal, or overtly paranoid. Their psychological problems have to be brought under control before they can comfortably integrate into a self-help support group.

Overly dependent people can drain everybody in the support group, including the facilitators. The severely dependent do not understand the principle of self-help. Their goal is to get someone to do it for them. There are always people who see themselves as just the ones who can help the dependent persons. These group members will burn themselves out in the process, become impatient with the individuals they thought they could fix, and unhappy with the facilitators for not using their skills to make the dependent persons better. Any suggestions made to encourage the dependent personalities will be met with a myriad of reasons why they cannot follow through. Groups not devoted to bereavement support are better able to cope with this type of problem.

The bereaved who attend a support group for the sole purpose of finding mates can be disruptive. However, if doing away with their single status is only one of the reasons they are in the group, it can work out for them and for the other participants. They may, in fact, find mates while dealing with their other bereavement related problems.

Health problems are common for participants in support groups. Their distress in having to manage them alone is one of the reasons that they need the support of the group. Participants who have health problems that are the focus of their lives need to get help from outside resources both for their physical problems and for their preoccupation with them. When they report a medical disaster every time they attend a session, the usually empathetic group members become impatient with their ongoing saga of increasingly poor health. They do not want to sit in attendance while the persistently unhealthy describe their latest excursion to the emergency room.

Some participants will have overwhelming family problems. They may be in situations in which they are being abused or exploited. In such a case, immediate action is needed. If those who are in these dangerous situations are unwilling to act on their own behalf, reports can be made to the abuse line and public officials will investigate. Again, as distressing as their plight may be, and as apparent as is their need for help, the urgency of the situation is not compatible with the aims of bereavement support groups. All available energy and concern goes to this type of problem, and mutual self-help is suspended. This causes too much stress for the individual group members. These problems need to be addressed individually or by groups established to support men and women in abusive situations.

Of course, there will be times when one of the participants will have a problem that monopolizes a group session. This is to be expected. But ongoing problems not related to a grief reaction are more appropriately handled through the authorities or agencies that routinely address those kinds of issues.

Problem Participants

Group participants have problems. They are of concern to the facilitators. It is for that reason that the sessions are being held. That is usual. Unfortunately, it is also usual that the group will contain problem participants, as well as participants with problems. These problem participants are in the appropriate place for the appropriate reason but express themselves in ways that unsettle the helping process of the group. The facilitators are charged with keeping the group on track by managing those participants who, by their words and actions, make a muddle. A list of major offenders follows, along with tactics that will help facilitate the forward movement of the group. Credit is given to Folken (1990a), Rubin & Rubin (1992), Vineyard (1990), and Worden (1991), for many of these conceptualizations.

Tangents The group member may start out on track. One thing reminds him of another, and before anyone can intervene, he is on another topic and moving fast. Participants that were interested start looking glassy eyed, small conversations break out among group members seated next to each other, some glance at their watches, and a few get caught up in the tangent.

1   The leader can wait for a word or statement that is related to the topic and jump in, wresting the floor from the talker.
2   The speaker can be asked, "What is your point?" There is danger in this, as it can send him off on another tangent.
3   "How is this germane to what we are discussing?" is a tactful way to let the speaker know that the facilitator is trying to stay on task.

4   When he pauses for breath, the leader can say, "Thank you for sharing that," and quickly ask a question of another participant or make a statement that returns the focus to the subject being discussed.

5   If the time is right, the leader can announce a break.

6   Pick up on anything the speaker is saying that might be constructive and build on it.

7   If the speaker touches on a topic that is relevant, write it on the board, telling the speaker and the group that it is time to continue with the subject at hand but that they will get back to the speaker's problem later in the session.

8   Ask the group if they want to talk about something the speaker brought up or go back to what was being discussed.

9   Simply say, "We're getting a little off course and we need to get back to _____."

10   Turn your back to the speaker and start writing something on the board that introduces a new topic.

Repeats the Same Story   The same story repeated during each session, with little variance from the original telling, aggravates the other group members and destroys their empathy and concern.

1   The facilitator can interrupt and ask questions. Did anything like this ever happen to you before? What did you do then? Have you discussed this with anyone else? What have others said to you? What is your most vivid memory about the deceased? These questions will redirect the speaker's thoughts and give the other participants a new slant on the story.

2   The facilitator may want to point out that the newly bereaved find it necessary to repeat the story of the death of the loved one (if this is the story being retold), as this helps them come to terms with the reality of the death, and that the bereaved in a support group are able to understand this.

3   Invite the rest of the group to participate in the story. Have any of them ever had a similar experience? What did they do about it? What were their feelings?

4   Approach the speaker privately and ask if she is having trouble moving beyond the incident she keeps repeating. She may decide to talk individually with the facilitator or make an appointment with a grief counselor.

Does Not Talk in the Group   Naturally reticent or shy people may sit quietly through group sessions. They end up being ignored, or the group members become uncomfortable with their silence. The introspective may be content to learn from the talking that others do. Shy people, on the other hand, develop more tension as time goes on and they cannot find an opening they deem appropriate for their sharing; they feel left out. The other group members are curious about them. They sometimes feel the silent ones are being disapproving or sitting in judgment. Because it is hard to decide whether the soundless are that way by choice or because of internal pressures, the facilitator notes who does not verbally contribute to the group and takes action to involve them.

1   When withdrawn people attend the group, incorporate them into the group by asking one or more questions that everyone is to answer. Go around the room, and ask every group member the same question. Do this in the first session that new participants attend, and do it in every session that includes people who do not normally speak up.

2   If nonverbal communication is noted, comment on it. Observe that the hushed participant appears to be distressed, looks as though he wants to talk, had a noticeable reaction to a statement, or appears involved in the topic. Ask him how he feels.

3   Pay attention each time the person who seldom speaks has something to offer. Reinforce what he says by acknowledging the offering. Refer to it on occasion if it can be used within the context of the dialogue. Give his words value.

Gripe Sessions   A gripe session is a splendid thing. It is astonishingly relaxing to complain with others who share the same grievances. However, ongoing gripe sessions that deteriorate into blame and recrimination are not helpful. They are depressing and paint a picture of a hostile world filled with unsympathetic people. Some legitimate gripes are acceptable. Constant griping is not.

1   If no participant comes up with an experience that puts a better light on the topic, present an anecdote that gives the group members a more favorable way of looking at the problem.

2   Summarize the gripes so the group members know that their discontent is heard. Then ask what anybody has done to solve the problem.

3   Ask if there are any positive approaches to the problem. If there are none, ask how they plan to live with the difficulties.

4   If one or two of the participants set the group tone with their constant gripes, snaring others in their unhappiness, confront them with questions about their participation in the problem. Did they do something to cause it, to make it worse? Have they done anything to improve the situation? Engage other members of the group in problem solving. If there are no suggestions from the group, the facilitator can make some.

5   Ask if the complainers had anything good happen to them during the week. If they say no, be more specific. Did they see anyone they liked? Did they get a letter from someone they are concerned about? Did they accomplish something? Was there any act of kindness directed their way?

Advice Giving   The advice giver has the answer to everybody's problems. These are not necessarily people who are authorities on everything, but people who want to help and who feel useful if they can solve other people's problems. Even though they are in the group to get help because they could not fix themselves, they are not deterred from making every effort to fix everybody else. When they hear that people are in pain, they jump in with advice on what they should do. If they use themselves as an example of the proper procedure, they do not do it in a sharing sense. They do it to point out that this is the way it should be done. Some advice-giving is appreciated. When another group member knows a good locksmith or has had experience in negotiating the legal system, the counsel is accepted because it provides information. That is different than prescribing how another should function.

1 Remind the advice giver of the rule against giving advice.
2 Thank the speaker for her report on how she would handle the situation, stating that her way may have worked for her, but everyone has their own way.
3 Ask the group members if any of them have tried the approach suggested.
4 Ask the group members to analyze the advice for possible good or bad consequences.
5 Speak to the recipients of the advice, explaining that all advice has to be evaluated. Advice can be accepted, modified, or ignored.
6 Ask the recipients of the advice if they had asked for advice. If they did, they got it free. Remind them that it was free and that that may be what it is worth to them—nothing. It is their decision.
7 Talk about advice in general. Most people who talk about their problems are not asking for advice. They are asking for someone to listen, try to understand, empathize, and share.
8 Discuss the danger of advice. If advice is given and taken, and it does not work out, the recipient of the advice blames the person who told her what to do. The person following the advice may thus decide not to take responsibility for her own actions.
9 Help the advice giver understand that people usually already know what they should do or what they did wrong. They do not need or want to be told.

Chronic Complainers   Complaining is not a bad thing. It is a validating activity when the complaint is shared by all present. A little goes a long way, however. The bereaved have many complaints in common. Their aim is to avoid getting caught up in complaints and help one another find their way out of the morass. The chronic complainers manage to find fault with everything and become real "downers" for the rest of the group members. Although the others recognize the complainers' negative approach to life, some of what they say is true; it sticks in the mind and spreads dissatisfaction. Complaining is disheartening and irritating when it is aimed at everything else, but downright frustrating when it is leveled at the facilitator and the functioning of the group.

1 Involve the group. Have them validate the complainer's experience with their own or give another version based on what they have done.

2   Ask the complainer what he has done about the situation.

3   Use the complainer's pronouncements as a stepping-stone to talking about ways to handle what cannot be changed or controlled.

4   Respond to legitimate complaints with positive and remedial ideas.

5   Listen carefully for anything that is even remotely positive and latch on to that. Reinforce the affirmative, and quickly move on before the complainer can point out how wrong you are.

6   Listen to the complaints and acknowledge that anger and irritation are normal reactions to loss.

7   Ask if something else is bothering him. What is making him so irritable.

Competitors   The competitors need the most of something. They want the most attention, have the worst problem, handle grief better than anyone else, or compete with the facilitator to be the group leader.

1   Do not be stingy with recognition. The competitor is obvious in pursuing it, be obvious in giving it.

2   Let the competitor help in the running of the group if she is in fact helpful. This person may have good ideas, know the right thing to say, and have examples and experiences that are close to profound. Just do not let her take the group away from the rest of the participants. The facilitator needs to keep enough control so that the needs of all the participants are met.

3   Point out that no one person's loss is worse than another person's loss. Everybody's loss is the worst because it is theirs. Everyone in the group suffers from loss.

Jokers   Humor in the face of adversity is helpful. When everything is turned into a joke, it is irritating. The group members, trying to pursue a serious discussion, will not welcome being waylaid with a humorous aside. Once in a while humor is acceptable, but continuous joking is disruptive and disrespectful.

1   Appreciate appropriate humor. Everybody needs it.

2   Ask the joker what she is feeling. Help her develop insight.

3   Say, "This is no joking matter."

4   Take the jokes seriously. Extract the distress from the humor and explore it further with the joker and with the rest of the group.

5   Discuss the value of humor as a defense. How is it helpful? When is it not helpful?

Irrelevant   The speakers who relate stories or information that seems to have no relation to the subject being discussed may be using irrelevance as a defense mechanism to keep from getting involved in painful material. It is not a good defense in a bereavement support group.

1   Say that you do not see the point. This is risky, however, as it might produce another irrelevant story.

2   Remark that these statements seem to be taking us afield, and return to the topic.

3   Say that the story is interesting and you would like to hear more, but you cannot allow yourself and the group to become involved because time is limited and there is much work to do. Then get back on track.

4   Comment that he or she might want to discuss that further during the break.

5   Point out that the individual's topic and concerns are important, but a bereavement support group is not the place for that particular discussion.

Overly Defensive   The overly defensive are ever alert to threats. They take everything personally. A suggestion, an unintentional slight, a minor mistake, or a well-intentioned response can bring out the defensiveness. The group members and facilitators are left wondering what they did. People become reluctant to talk to the defensive person for fear of hurting her feelings or having to listen to her defend herself.

1   Use reality testing. Ask what was said or done that made her feel that way.

2   Interrupt the stream of defensiveness by asking the previous speakers if that is what they meant and giving them an opportunity to clarify.

3   Preface every statement with, "Don't take this personally."

4   Make a blanket statement that we are all on the same side.

End-Sharing   The end-sharers are those who give no indication of a pressing problem throughout the group session. Just before quitting time, however, they bring up a difficulty and ask for help.

1   The first time the end-sharer asks the group for help as they are ready to leave, the facilitator can ask if anybody wants to stay to continue the discussion for 15 more minutes. Some will stay. Give the full 15 minutes and then wrap up.

2   If end-sharing continues, explain that it is the facilitator's obligation to close the group on time, but that the problem has been noted and will be the first thing on the agenda at the next meeting.

3   The facilitator may agree to stay and briefly discuss the problem with the end-sharer.

4   The facilitator acknowledges that the individual has an important problem, and asks him to call the facilitator sometime during the week so they can talk about it.

5   Ask if anybody in the group is able to volunteer to discuss this problem with the problem participant sometime between sessions.

6 Assign the end-sharer homework. Ask him to write out the problem, what has been done about it so far, and what may be some possible approaches, and bring this to the next session of the group.

7 Ask the group 15 or 20 minutes before the ending time of the session whether anybody has anything that needs to be covered before the next meeting. If a notorious end-sharer is in the group, make a point of asking him in particular.

Subsets In ongoing groups, and less frequently in closed-end groups, people socialize outside the group and get involved in each others lives. This is a good by-product of the support group experience. It is not good for the therapeutic aspects of the group if these subsets are active during the group sessions. When they talk about their avocational activities, laugh at inside jokes, and flaunt their extracurricular relationships, the others feel left out. It is divisive and annoying. The facilitators do not want to dampen the social life of the group members; neither do the leaders want the subset's social life to be part of the group process. There are some tactics the group leader can use.

1 Announce that it is nice to have friends and good times, but that mysterious asides have no place in a support group.

2 Ask if they want to talk about their social life in the group or reserve the group for matters relating to bereavement.

3 Ask the subset if their references to what they do outside the group pertain to acknowledging their progress and motivating others to find interesting pursuits for themselves.

4 Suggest that matters that exclude some members of the support group should not be brought up by other members.

5 The leaders can involve themselves in the conversation and extract anything that bears on grief reduction. Is there an activity to recommend? Was it hard to manage socially as a single person? What barriers did they have to overcome to do some of the things they are doing? Do they have any comments on the value of new friendships and activities?

Own Agenda Everybody goes to a bereavement support group to find relief from the pain of grief, but sometimes that does not appear to be the case. Now and again, participants will have their own or a hidden agenda. Sometimes the agenda is so well hidden that they themselves do not know what it is. The group members and the facilitators just know that they are "out of sync" with the group. Sometimes these agendas work out all right in time. The participants who come to prove that they do not need help, or to find help for someone else, will find that that does not work. They will become integrated into the group, seeking comfort for their own concerns, or will leave because the group does not offer what they want. If someone has a personal agenda and is open about it, it can be addressed. They then stay for what they can get out of the group, or they go where they can more appropriately find what they want. It is the people whose agendas are kept secret and who try to undermine the group that produce a miserable situation.

1   Accept the participant's statement without comment. This does not reinforce what she says, nor does it open up the person's agenda for elaboration or challenge.
2   Speak to her alone after the session or by telephone in an effort to find out what the participant wants from the group.
3   Look for clues. When one is found, ask if the participant wants the group to address that problem, explain that this group is not appropriate for that activity, or suggest other places and services that are available in the community.
4   Co-opt the participant. Get her involved in the success of the group by giving her an assignment. The person can be asked to research something, provide something, or be part of a special project. This technique topples the participant's agenda. She becomes a group supporter.

Boring Speakers   Maybe it is the tone of voice or the use of words. Perhaps it is the subject they are talking about or their body language. Whatever it is, it is boring. The topic may be appropriate and the words sincere, but the speaker is boring. He or she goes on and on and gets lost in detail. The point gets lost as does the audience.

1   Summarize and move on.
2   Ask the speaker to state the problem as though writing a headline for the newspaper. Say that you want to see it in big black letters.
3   Speak to the person after the session and let him tell you the entire story. Make sure the person knows that you hear and understand. Hope that that frees him from having to tell it to you again, or bringing it up in the group.
4   Say, "Let me see if I understand this," state his point succinctly, and ask for comments from the other group members.
5   Say, "Let me help you," and state the point for him.
6   Admit that he is losing you in the detail.
7   Point out that the details are not important, what he did and how he felt are what the group members want to hear.

Know-It-All   If anybody is an expert on grief, it is the individual who is going through it or has survived it. Self-appointed experts on everybody's grief deny the other group members their own experiences. They have all the answers to the grief process and to everything else. As helpful as it may be to have resident experts, it cannot be assumed that they are experts on anything but letting other people know that they think they know it all.

1   Acknowledge the know-it-all as a good resource. Then ask for other ideas and experiences.

2   Label the comments a point of view or an opinion, rather than make it a right-or-wrong issue.

3   Give the person credit for a good thought, and solicit other thoughts from the other participants.

4   Do not precipitate a showdown. Always consider the person's suggestions.

Everybody Talking at Once   Chaos or a spirited discussion? Maybe a little of both. When everybody is talking at once, or talking with each other instead of with the group, the process disintegrates.

1   Start writing on the board. Channel the comments toward the facilitator by writing out one thought at a time.

2   Suggest that it is time for most of us to listen while one person talks.

3   Have a prearranged signal, and use it. Ring a bell, clap your hands.

4   Announce a break.

5   Get the participants' attention and announce a new topic.

Negative Body Language   The participants look so uncomfortable that they are making the facilitators and the group members uncomfortable. Are they in pain, disapproving, hostile?

1   The facilitator may want to ask, "You look (uncomfortable, unhappy). What is wrong?"

2   Simply say, "Are you OK?"

Monopolizes the Discussion   The goal is for everyone to verbalize equally. Of course this goal is never attained, as people verbalize differently. Participants are in all ranges of the spectrum, from the very quiet to the very talkative. As much as facilitators welcome verbal participants, those who talk all the time are a problem.

1   Give the overtalker a compliment on what was said, and move on.

2   Interrupt and say, "Let's hear what the others have to say."

3   Refresh the person's memory about the equal-air-time rule.

4   Say, "We have to stop there, as that is interesting and worthy of discussion by the rest of us."

5   Use body language. Hold up your hand to signal stop. Touch the loquacious participant to get his attention.

6   Ask the person to take his turn at listening.

7   Grab onto a relevant phrase or thought, and throw it out for discussion.

8   Signal that it is time for a stretch before we move on.

9   Tell the individual that he is a good participator, and now we need to get others involved.

Individuals make up the group, but the group helps the individuals. To make the group work as intended, certain individuals will need help to become contributing parts of the system. The facilitators constantly have to keep a balance between the needs of the individuals and the needs of the group. It is exciting, challenging, and well worth the effort.

Chapter 9

After All Is Said And Done

A perfect grief group attended by perfect mourners is beyond the reach of the facilitators and the grievers. There are too many complications wrought by personal characteristics, experiences, and beliefs; cultural mores, values, and traditions; and environmental pressures, changes, and incidents. Considering these exigencies, it is a tribute to everyone's good work and determination that group facilitators are able to help the bereaved, and the bereaved are able to make use of the proffered assistance.

Today the necessity of grieving is readily acknowledged by most professionals and much of the population. The pioneers in death education and counseling began their work over two decades ago. Literature was sparse, conferences were few, many thought the subject did not apply to them. The bereaved, however, knew that they could not conform to society's expectation of a brief surcease from the demands of every day life and a rapid return to normality. They handled this obligation by pretending, by getting physically or mentally sick, by finding supportive people, by blunting their feelings with drugs, work, sex, or some replacement that took their time, drained their energy, and distracted their thoughts. Then as now, some of the bereaved looked for support from people who had been there. Others preferred to acknowledge their pain privately and struggle on alone. The bereaved coped without the help that is now available. Many continue to do so. But they do not have to. There are books, magazine articles, government publications, television programs, movies, classes, volunteer organizations, and a range of professional services competing for their attention. Personal observation, anecdotal material, and the many studies cited previously in this book have shown the effectiveness of bereavement support services.

Once the reality of grief was avowed, a plethora of bereavement services became available. Bereavement was identified as a normal process bringing some predictable problems and feelings that could be survived and survived well. As much as the pain of loss was seen as universal, it was also seen as unique. Loss and grief happened to everybody, but everybody had their own feelings and coping mechanisms. There was not a single bereavement model, and there could not be just one helpful approach. No one approach fits all. One-to-one is more effective for some people; group for others. Between these options there are variations. Bereavement groups come in all sizes and descriptions and appeal to the bereaved in different ways. The group the bereaved chooses will depend not only on what is available at the time it is needed, but also on what suits. Depending on their usual method of dealing with problems, the bereaved will be attracted to different types of groups. The action oriented will look for groups that offer activities, projects, and causes. The cerebral types will go to classes and seminars, and want to learn more about the process and how to handle it. People who prefer socializing will pick parties, potlucks, and luncheon meetings. A good many will want to talk to others who are also experiencing loss, welcoming the opportunity to share thoughts and feelings. As the bereaved decide they need more or different support than can be given by family, friends, neighbors, and religious organizations, they will decide to attend bereavement support groups that they feel are responsive to their needs.

At first ardently asserted by activists who were responding to personal knowledge, and now verified by research, is the fact that the mind and the body are linked (Hiratsuka, 1994). Because bereavement groups help restore equilibrium and hope, and reduce stress, fear, worry, and depression, the natural body defenses against disease are able to do work as designed, preventing physical as well as emotional distress. This occurs because of the inherent support in any bereavement group. The bereaved may participate in groups hoping to find friends, interests, or entertainment. They will also find support.

Offering variety gets the word out on the availability of bereavement support groups. If the bereaved sign up for a seminar, they will learn of other services, talk with people undergoing similar adjustments, and may resolve that they too can benefit from other types of support, such as the traditional sit-down-and-talk-about-it group.

The bereaved who have always attacked problems will attack their bereavement in the same way. They will find what is available in the community and make use of it. Untold numbers of the bereaved, however, are not knowledgeable about bereavement support, do not know what is being offered in the area, and are too fatigued and distressed to search. That is why advertising is important. It pays off in increased numbers of survivors attending bereavement support groups and more people assisted in their adjustments to their lives without their loved ones.

LET PEOPLE KNOW

Advertisement must go on unceasingly. One mode is not enough. The only way to find out what works is to try all the media. Make contact through homeowners' associations; reach people through seminars, classes, and speeches; and distribute printed material in all directions and to every possible resource. Dare to be creative without being outrageous. Put some "oomph" into the written message by combining color, interesting copy, and dynamic illustrations. Make sure that there are no pockets of population left uninformed.

Advertise the service by giving good service. Guarantee courtesy and consideration to each person at each contact. Follow through, and follow up. If anyone must be turned away, be sure that that person is offered alternative services or referred for help from a more appropriate resource. Let the people who are accepted into the program know that they and their business are important, that it is a mutual undertaking, and that every effort will be made to respond to their needs (Sewell & Brown, 1990).

THE FACILITATORS CONTRIBUTE AND LEARN

Conscientious and astute facilitators never take the bereaved or the group for granted. Every session is a production number. The choreography is always carefully completed. The facilitators know that they will always learn more from the participants than they will teach, but they nevertheless need a sound background in group dynamics and grief and loss issues. Because the facilitators are sure that the bereavement support group is a valuable adjunct to a constructive grief process, they are never bored, are always excited by the progress manifested by the group's graduates, and are in awe of the power of the combined contributions of the participants. As a consequence, they do not find the job depressing or tedious. It is very satisfying to be able to help.

Cohesive groups function best. They are more gratifying for the participants, easier to facilitate, and produce the best results (Sarri & Galinsky, 1967). The bereaved who have suffered similar kinds of losses, such as the death of a parent, spouse, or child or, more specifically a murdered child, a death from AIDS or suicide or cancer, appreciate being in groups with people who have been through the same ordeal. Similarity leads to cohesion, which equals successful support groups. Although the ideal may not be attainable because the area is too thinly populated to sustain specialized groups, it is helpful to keep the specific needs of certain bereaved populations in mind. They can attend a mixed group but be given reading material, individual recognition for problems specific to their losses, or referrals to other community resources that might be useful and put in touch with national organizations that cater to their particular grief.

Bereavement Groups are not for Everyone

Some prospective participants will be in such severe pain, have so many ancillary problems, and be so immobilized that they will demoralize an entire support group. They deplete the other participants and still are so overwhelmed that hopelessness prevails. These bereaved need specialized, one-to-one assistance from the community agencies that can address their situations. If someone so needy gets into the group, the facilitators also become frustrated as their attempts at redirection are of no avail. They will have to move to get the participant the needed help and save the group. But the disturbing participant cannot just disappear, never to be heard of again. The rest of the group members have gotten involved; they are captivated by the story and will have to know the ending. With the participant's permission, the facilitators should explain that the participant has been put in touch with the people or places that can administer the necessary assistance.

Screening is a tool for preventing group disruption. It is better to find the right place for unsettling applicants before they become entangled with the group members. If facilitators do not know who is not suitable for support groups, they will learn soon enough, if only from reading the participants' evaluations. The participants will invariably complain about the individual who monopolized the group, did not seem to understand its purpose, or did not conform in some important way. The very demanding participants or the overwhelmed ones may not be mentioned on the evaluation forms, but the participants will ask about them when they run into the facilitator once the group has disbanded. This is a clear indication that those members were a troubling presence.

CONCLUSION

A group is a delicate entity in that it is affected by everyone's personality and behavior, but it is not so delicate that it is unable to integrate diversity and respond to circumstances that demand more time and attention than is generally allocated to each participant. Group members are responsive. This is one of the qualities that makes a bereavement group supportive. It is expected that the facilitators also will be responsive. Ignoring a problem seldom works. The group members know it is there and grow troubled if it is not recognized and discussed. No matter how cohesive the group, how long it has been in operation, or how much the participants appreciate their leaders, they still will anticipate that the facilitators will do the right thing and handle any group problem. Bereavement support group members do not attend to effect personality changes, to struggle with difficult people, or to diagnose and modify unpleasant character traits. They attend to learn to live in a world from which their loved ones are missing. They want to give and receive support, not work on their, or anyone's problems, that are more productively addressed in psychotherapy. Bereavement support groups cannot be all things to all people, but they can provide a very important service to the people whose needs they are designed to meet.

Facilitating a support group is intrinsically rewarding. As the bereaved learn and grow, so do the facilitators. Admiration and appreciation are mutual. The leaders have the humbling experience of being with the participants during a crucial and soul-searing time in their lives and are a part of their triumphant journey out of despair.

Book Bibliographies for Support Group Participants

BOOKS FOR ADULTS

Bozarth, A.R. (1982). *Life is goodby, life is hello: Grieving well through all kinds of loss.* Minneapolis, MN: Compcare.

Brocks, A.M. (1985). *The grieving time: A year's account of recovery from loss.* New York: Harmony.

Cole, D. (1992). *After great pain: A new life emerges.* New York: Summit.

Colgrove, M., Bloomfield, H.H., & McWilliams, P. (1976). *How to survive the loss of a love.* New York: Bantam.

Davidson, G. (1984). *Understanding mourning: A guide for those who grieve.* Minneapolis, MN: Augsburg.

Davies, P. (1988). *Grief: Climb toward understanding.* New York: Carol Communications.

Gaver, J.R. (1976). *A guide book for widows and widowers.* New York: Belmont Tower.

Grollman, E.A. (1977). *Living when a loved one has died.* Boston, MA: Beacon.

Jacobsen, G.B. (1990). *Write grief—How to transform loss with writing.* Menominee Falls, WI: McCormick & Schilling.

James, J.W., & Cherry, F. (1988). *The grief recovery handbook.* New York: Harper Perennial.

Kramer, H., & Kramer, K. (1993). *Conversations at midnight.* New York: William Morrow.

Kübler-Ross, E. (1969). *On death and dying.* New York: Macmillan.

Kübler-Ross, E. (1974). *Questions and answers on death and dying.* New York: Macmillan.

Kübler-Ross, E. (Ed.). (1975). *Death: The final stage of growth.* Englewood Cliffs, NJ: Prentice-Hall.

Kübler-Ross, E. (1981). *Living with death and dying.* New York: Macmillan.

Kushner, H.S. (1983). *When bad things happen to good people.* New York: Avon.

Levine, S. (1987). *Healing into life and death.* Garden City, NY: Doubleday.

Lewis, C.S. (1963). *A grief observed.* New York: Seabury.

Lord, J.H. (1987). *No time for goodbyes.* Ventura, CA: Pathfinder.

Manning, D. (1981). *Don't take my grief away from me.* Springfield, IL: Creative Marketing.

Neeld, E.H. (1990). *Seven choices.* New York: Clarkson N. Potter.

O'Connor, N. (1984). *Letting go with love: The grieving process.* Tucson, AZ: La Mariposa.

Palmer, E., & Watt, J. (1987). *Living and working with bereavement.* Calgary, Alberta: Deselig Enterprises.

Potts, N. (1978). *Loneliness: Living between the times.* Wheaton, IL: Victor.

Price, E. (1982). *Getting through the night.* New York: Dial Press.

Rando, T. (1991). *How to go on living when someone you love dies.* New York: Bantam.

Sanders, C.M. (1989). *Grief: The mourning after.* New York: John Wiley & Sons.

Schiff, H.S. (1986). *Living through mourning: Finding comfort and hope when a loved one has died.* New York: Viking.

Staudacher, C. (1987). *Beyond grief: A guide for recovering from the death of a loved one.* Oakland, CA: New Harbinger.

Stearns, A.K. (1984). *Living through personal crisis.* Chicago, IL: Thomas More.

Tatelbaum, J. (1989). *You don't have to suffer.* New York: Harper & Row.

Temes, R. (1984). *Living with an empty chair.* New York: Irvington.

Viscott, D. (1977). *Risking.* New York: Pocket.

Weenolsen, P. (1988). *Transcendence of loss over the life span.* New York: Hemisphere.

Wolfelt, A.D. (1992). *Understanding grief: Helping yourself heal.* Muncie, IN: Accelerated Development.

BOOKS FOR ADULTS WHOSE PARENTS HAVE DIED

Angel, M.D. (1987). *The orphaned adult: Confronting the death of a parent.* New York: Insight.
Myers, E. (1986). *When parents die: A guide for adults.* New York: Viking.

BOOKS ON DISENFRANCHISED DEATH

Doka, K. J. (Ed.). (1989). *Disenfranchised grief.* New York: Lexington.
Hewitt, J. (1980). *After suicide.* Philadelphia: Westminster.

BOOKS FOR YOUNG WIDOWS

Blankenship, J. (1984). *In the center of the night.* New York: PaperJacks.

BOOKS FOR WIDOWS

Armstrong, A., & Donohue, M.R. (1993). *On your own: A widow's passage to emotional and financial well-being.* Dearborn, MI: Dearborn Financial.
Caine, L. (1974). *Widow.* New York: William Morrow.
Gates, P. (1990). *Suddenly alone: A woman's guide to widowhood.* New York: Harper & Row.
Ginsburg, G. (1991). *When you've become a widow.* Los Angeles: Jeremy P. Tarcher.

BOOKS FOR WIDOWERS

Campbell, S., & Silverman, P. (1987) *Widower: When men are left alone.* New York: Prentice Hall.
Elmer, L. (1987). *Why her why now: A man's journey through love and death and grief.* New York: Bantam.
Staudacher, C. (1991). *Men and grief.* Oakland, CA: New Harbinger.

BOOKS FOR THE WIDOWED

DiGiulio, R.C. (1989). *Beyond widowhood: From bereavement to emergence and hope.* New York: The Free Press.
Shuchter, S.R. (1986). *Dimensions of grief: Adjusting to the death of a spouse.* San Francisco: Jossey-Bass.

BOOKS FOR CHILDREN

Adler, C.S. (1990). *Ghost brother.* New York: Clarion.
Boulden, Jim. (1989). *Saying goodbye activity book.* Santa Rosa, CA: Author.

Bourne, G., & Meier, J. (1988). *What is happening?* Milwaukee, WI: St. Luke's Medical Center.

Clardy, A. (1984). *Dusty was my friend.* New York: Human Sciences.

Gravelle, K., & Hoskins, C. (1989). *Teenagers face to face with bereavement.* Englewood Cliffs, NJ: J. Messner.

Grollman, E.A. (1993). *Straight talk about death for teenagers.* Boston: Beacon.

Keller, H. (1987). *Goodby, Max.* New York: Greenwillow.

LeShan, E.J. (1976). *Learning to say good-bye: When a parent dies.* New York: Macmillan.

Mann, P. (1977). *There are two kinds of terrible.* New York: Atheneum.

Naughton, J. (1989). *My brother stealing second.* New York: Harper & Row.

Richter, E. (1986). *Losing someone you love: When a brother or sister dies.* New York: G.P. Putnam's.

Rogers, F. (1988). *When a pet dies.* New York: G.P. Putnam's.

Sharmat, M.W. (1977). *I don't care.* New York: Macmillan.

Simon, N. (1979). *We remember Phillip.* Chicago: A. Whitman.

Stein, S.B. (1974). *About dying.* New York: Walker.

Wright, B.R. (1991). *The cat next door.* New York: Holiday House.

BOOKS FOR CHILDREN'S HELPERS

Alderman, L. (1989). *Why did daddy die?: Helping children cope with the loss of a parent.* New York: Pocket.

Fitzgerald, H. (1992). *The grieving child: A parents' guide.* New York: Simon & Schuster.

Gaffney, D. (1988). *The seasons of grief: Helping children grow through loss.* New York: Penguin.

Grollman, E.A. (Ed.). (1967). *Explaining death to children.* Boston: Beacon.

Grollman, E.A. (1990). *Talking about death: A dialogue between parent and child* (rev. ed.). Boston: Beacon.

Kübler-Ross, E. (1983). *On children and death.* New York: Macmillan.

Linn, E. (1990). *150 facts about grieving children.* Incline Village, NV: The Publisher's Mark.

Schaefer, D., & Lyons, C. (1986). *How do we tell the Children?: A parents' guide to helping children understand and cope when someone dies.* New York: Newmarket.

Van Ornum, W., & Mordock, J.B. (1990). *Crisis counseling with children and adolescents: A guide for nonprofessional counselors.* New York: Continuum.

Wass, H., & Coor, C.A. (1984). *Helping children cope with death: Guidelines and resources* (rev. ed.). Washington, DC: Hemisphere.

Wolfelt, A.D. (1983). *Helping children cope with grief.* Muncie, IN: Accelerated Development.

BOOKS FOR PARENTS

Berezin, N. (1982). *After a loss in pregnancy: Help for families affected by a miscarriage, a stillbirth, or the loss of a newborn.* New York: Simon & Schuster.

DeFrain, J., Taylor, J., & Ernest, L. (1982). *Coping with sudden infant death.* Lexington, MA: D.C. Heath.

Donnelly, K.F. (1982). *Recovering from the loss of a child.* New York: Macmillan.

Friedman, R., & Goradstein, B. (1982). *Surviving pregnancy loss.* Boston: Little, Brown.

Johnson, J., & Johnson, M. (1989). *Dear parents, letters to bereaved parents.* Omaha, NE: Centering Corporation.

Peppers, L.G., & Knapp, R. J. (1985). *How to go on living after the death of a baby.* Atlanta, GA: Peachtree.

Schwiebert, P., & Kirk, P. *When hello means goodbye.* Portland, OR: Perinatal Loss.

Schiff, H.S. (1977). *The bereaved parent.* New York: Penguin.

Seiden, O. J., & Timmons, M. J. (1984). *Coping with miscarriage.* Blue Ridge Summit, PA: Tab.

Toder, F. (1986). *When your child is gone: Learning to live again.* Sacramento, CA: Capital.

References

American Association of Retired Persons. (1986). *Public relations manual for program volunteers* (PF 3814(986)-D 12584). Washington, DC: Author.

American Association of Retired Persons. (1988). *On being alone.* Washington, DC: Author.

American Psychiatric Association. (1987). *Diagnostic and statistical manual* (3rd ed. revised). Washington, DC: Author.

Ariés, P. (1981). *The hour of our death.* New York: Alfred A. Knopf.

Atchley, R. C. (1975). Dimensions of widowhood in later life. *The Gerontologist, 15,* 176-178.

Atchley, R. C. (1988). *Social forces and aging* (5th ed.). (pp. 221-237). Belmont, CA: Wadsworth.

Baldwin, K. S. (1993). *Taking the time you need to grieve your loss.* St. Meinrad, IN: Abbey.

Barrett, C. J. (1978). Effectiveness of widow's groups in facilitating change. *Journal of Consulting and Clinical Psychology, 46,* 20-31.

Bartlett, B., & Radabaugh, S. (1987). Using the media to educate, recruit, and reach out. *Post Conference Report of Widowed Persons Servcie Tenth National Conference, October,* 30-33.

Bell, R., (1971). *Marriage and family interaction.* Homewood, IL: Dorsey Press.

Berardo, F. M. (1968). Widowhood status in the U.S.: Perspectives on a neglected aspect of the family life cycle. *The Family Coordinator, 17,* 191-203.

Berardo, F. M. (1970). Survivorship and social isolation: The case of the aged widower. *The Family Coordinator, 19,* 11-15.

Berezin, N. (1982). *After a loss in pregancy: Help for families affected by a miscarriage, a stillbirth, or the loss of a newborn.* New York: Simon and Schuster.

Blackshear, M. (1993, April). *How to build a multi-service bereavement program in a funeral home setting.* Paper presented at the Association for Death Education and Counseling conference, Memphis, TN.

Blau, Z. S. (1961). Structural constraints on friendship in old age. *American Sociologial Review, 26,* 429-439.

Bowlby, J. (1960). Grief and mourning in infancy and early childhood. *The Psychoanalytic Study of the Child, 15,* 9-52.

Bowlby, J. (1980). *Attachment and loss: Loss, sadness, and depression* (Vol. 3). New York: Basic.

Briese, P., & Farra, R. R. (1984). Men in crisis. *Post Conference Report of Widowed Persons Service Seventh National Conference,* 82. Washington, DC: AARP Widowed Persons Service.

Brothers, J. (1990). For the first year after Milt died, I lived in the past. *Good Housekeeping, November,* 163-233.

Brown, G. W. (1982). Early loss and depression. In C. M. Parkes and J. Stevenson-Hinde (Eds.), *The place of attachment in human behavior* (pp. 232-268). New York: Basic.

Caine, L. (1974). Breaking the silence. *Widow* (pp. 135-143). New York: William Morrow.

Campbell, S., & Silverman, P. R. (1987). What happens to men when their mates die. *Widower* (pp. 1-9). New York: Prentice Hall.

Chmurski, J. M. (1990, summer). Claudia. *Thanatos,* (pp. 12-13).

Cole, D. (1992). *After great pain: A new life emerges.* New York: Summit.

Corey, C. (1990). *Manual for theory and practice of group counseling.* Pacific Grove, CA: Brooks-Cole.

Crenshaw, D. A. (1990). A listing of some helping resources & Helping pre-school children, grade school children, adolescents to grieve. *Bereavement* (pp. 40-138; 171-173). New York: Continuum.

Crenshaw, D. A. (1990). The need to grieve throughout the life cycle. *Bereavement: Counseling the grieving through the life cycle.* (pp. 19-39). New York: Continuum.

Critical Incident Stress Debriefers of Florida, Inc. (1989). *State protocols & procedures manual.* Tallahassee, FL: Author.

Department of Health and Human Services. (1981). *Hospice education program for nurses* (DHHA Publication No. HRA 81-27). Washington, DC: U.S. Government Printing Office.

Dickson, C. (1990, October). Delivering a video message? Here's how to face the camera with confidence and credibility. *Training & Development Journal,* (pp. 79-82).

DiGiulio, R. C. (1989). Mutual support groups. *Beyond widowhood: From bereavement to emergence and hope* (pp. 145-158). New York: Free Press.

Dorsel, S. J., & Dorsel, T. N. (1986, Jan./Feb.). Helping parents whose child has died: A review of coping strategies and alternatives for support. *The American Journal of Hospice Care,* (pp. 17-20).

Duff, R. S., & Campbell, A. G. M. (1980). Moral and ethical dilemmas: Seven years into the debate about human ambiguity. *The Annals: The Social Meaning of Death, 447,* 19-28.

Engel, G. (1961). Is grief a disease? A challenge for medical research. *Psychosomatic Medicine, 23,* 18-23.

Farra, R. R. (1986). *Widowed persons service guide for trainers* (pp. 2-17). Washington, DC: American Association of Retired Persons.

Fenichel, O. (1945). *The psychoanalytic theory of neurosis.* New York: Norton.

Fitzgerald, H. (1992). *The grieving child: A parent's guide.* New York: Simon & Schuster.

Fitzgerald, H. (1993, April). *An educational/support group model for children.* Paper presented at the meeting of the Association for Death Education and Counseling, Memphis, TN.

Folken, M. H. (1991, March). *Bereavement support groups.* Paper presented at the Widowed Persons Service trainers and organizers meeting, Alexandria, VA.

Folken, M. H. (1990a, October). *Group dynamics.* Paper presented at the meeting of the Widowed Persons Service, Atlanta, GA.

Folken, M. H. (1990b). Moderating grief of widowed people in talk groups. *Death Studies, 14,* 171-176.

Fox, S. S. (1985). Children's healthy responses to the death of a parent or grandparent. *Post Conference Report of the Widowed Persons Service Eighth National Conference,* 109-115. Washington, DC: AARP Widowed Persons Service.

Freeman, L. (1990). When self-esteem replaces rage. *Our inner world of rage* (pp. 143-153). New York: Continuum.

Freud, A., & Burlingham, D. (1942). *War and children.* New York: International Universities Press.

Freud, S. (1961). Mourning and meloncholia. In J. Stradray (Ed. and Trans.), *The Standard Edition of the Complete Works of Sigmund Freud* (Vol. 14). New York: W. W. N orton. (Original work published in 1917).

Furman, R. (1964). Death and the young child. *The Psychoanalytic Study of the Child, 19,* 321-332.

Galinsky, M. J., & Schopler, J. H. (1977). Warning: Groups may be dangerous. *Social Work, 22,* 89-94.

Galinsky, M. J., & Schopler, J. H. (1981). When groups go wrong. *Social Work, 26,* 424-429.

Garvin, C. D. (1974). Group process: Usage and uses in social work practice. In P. Glasser, R. Sarri, & R. Vinter (Eds.), *Individual change through small groups* (pp. 209-232). New York: Free Press.

Gaver, J. R. (1976). There is no easy way ahead & Learning to be alive again. *Widows & widowers: All the wise and wherefores* (pp. 37-55). New York: Belmont Tower.

Glick, I. O., Weiss, R. S., & Parkes, C. M. (1974). *The first year of bereavement.* New York: Wiley.

Gorer, G. (1965). *Death, grief, and mourning.* Garden City, NY: Doubleday.

Haan, L. (1991, October). *Men in grief.* Paper presented at the Widowed Persons Service National Conference, Chicago, IL.

Haasl, B. S., & Marnocha, J. (1990). *Bereavement support group program for children.* Muncie, IN: Accelerated Development.

Hiratsuka, J. (1994, March). Mind-body wellness link probed. *NASW News,* 1.

Hughes, M. (1988). Defense mechanisms. *Mental health problems and the nursing home resident* (pp. 67-89). Texas: M & H.

Hughes, M. (1993). *Quick fixes: 303 ways to help yourself before the therapist arrives.* New York: Crossroad.

Johnson, C. (1974). Planning for termination of the group. In P. Glasser, R. Sarri, & R. Vinter (Eds.), *Individual change through the small groups* (pp. 258-265). New York: Free Press.

Jonas, A. R. (1983, May). Surviving a relative's murder. *Psychology Today,* pp. 14-15.

Kastenbaum, R. (1967). The child's understanding of death: How does it develop? In E. A. Grollman (Ed.), *Explaining death to children* (pp. 89-108). Boston: Beacon.

Kelly, J. (1985). Public relations. *Post Conference Report of Widowed Persons Service Eighth National Conference,* October, 139-143. Washington, DC: AARP Widowed Persons Service.

Klass, D. (1982). Self-help groups for the bereaved: Theory, theology, and practice. *Journal of Religion and Health, 21,* 307-323.

Klein, M. (1940). Mourning and its relation to manic-depressive states. *Contributions to psychoanalysis* 1921-1945, New York: Hillary.

Knapp, R. J. (1986). *Beyond endurance: When a child dies.* New York: Schocken Books.

Kübler-Ross, E. (1969). *On death and dying.* New York: Macmillan.

Kübler-Ross, E. (1974). Sudden death. *Questions and answers on death and dying* (pp. 60-73). New York: Macmillan.

Kübler-Ross, E. (1983). *On children and death.* New York: Macmillan.

Kushner, H. S. (1981). Sometimes there is no reason. *When bad things happen to good people* (pp. 46-55). New York: Avon.

Lazare, A. (1979) Unresolved grief. In A. Lazare (Ed.), *Outpatient psychiatry: Diagnosis and treatment* (p. 507). Baltimore: Williams and Wilkins.

Lindeman, B. (1983, July-Aug.). We were suddenly alone. *Dynamic Years,* pp. 48-54.

Lindemann, E. (1944). Symptomatology and management of acute grief. *American Journal of Psychiatry, 101,* 141-148.

Loewinsohn, R. J. (1979). I've become a person again. *Survival handbook for widows* (pp. 119-134). Chicago: Follett.

Lopata, H. (1973). *Widowhood in an American city.* Cambridge, MA: Schenckman Books.

Madara, E. J., & Meese, A. (1986). *The self-help sourcebook: Finding and forming mutual aid self-help groups.* Denville, NJ: St. Clares-Riverside Foundation.

Marris, P. (1958). *Widows and their families.* London: Routledge & Kegan Paul.

Marvel, M. G. (1992). Disenfranchised grief. *WPS Insights, 44,* 1-2.

Masson, R. L., & Jacobs, E. (1980, September). Group leadership: Practical points for beginners. *The Personnel and Guidance Journal,* pp. 52-55.

McGoldrick, M. (1991). Echoes from the past: Helping families mourn their losses. In F. Walsh & M. McGoldrick (Eds.), *Living beyond loss: Death in the family* (pp. 50-78). New York: Norton.

McKendree, D. J. (1989). *The spiral of grief: Coping with your loss.* Evanston, IL: NSM Resources.

Monahan, J. (1993, April). *A different kind of bereavement group.* Paper presented at the Association for Death Education and Counseling Conference, Memphis, TN.

Monson, L. (1985). Widowers. *Post Conference Report of the Widowed Persons Service Eighth National Conference, October,* 68-71. Washington, DC: AARP Widowed Persons Service.

Munneke, E., Foster, B., & Stombaugh, M. (1986). Support and nurturance of outreach volunteers. *Post Conference Report of the Widowed Persons Service Ninth National Conference, October,* 38-43. Washington, DC: AARP Widowed Persons Service.

Nagy, M. (1948). The child's theories concerning death. *Journal of Genetics and Psychology, 73,* 3-27.

National Institute of Mental Health. (1979). *Talking to children about death.* (DHEW Publication No. ADM 79-838). Washington, DC: U.S. Government Printing Office.

Neeld, E. H. (1990). *Seven choices.* New York: Clarkson N. Potter.

Nelson, P. (1989, spring). Educating children about death as well as life. *Thanatos,* p. 2.

Nichols, R., & Nichols, J. (1975). Funerals: A time for grief and growth. In E. Kübler-Ross (Ed.), *Death: The final stage of growth* (pp. 81-96). Englewood Cliffs, NJ: Prentice-Hall.

Novack, D. (1979). Changes in physicians' attitudes toward telling the cancer patient. *Journal of the American Medical Association, 421,* 897-900.

Nudel, A. R. (1986). Younger widowed. *Post Conference Report of the Widowed Persons Service Ninth National Conference, October,* 89-91. Washington, DC: AARP Widowed Persons Service.

Nudel, A. R. (1987). Do's and don't's of support groups. *Post Conference Report of the Widowed Persons Service Tenth National Conference, October,* 70-72. Washington, DC: AARP Widowed Persons Service.

Obershaw, R. (1985). Myths about grieving. *Post Conference Report of the Widowed Persons Service Eighth National Conference,* 2-3. Washington, DC: AARP Widowed Persons Service.

O'Connor, N. (1984). *Letting go with love: The grieving process.* Tucson, AZ: La Mariposa.

Oken, D. (1961). What to tell cancer patients-A study of medical attitudes. *Journal of the American Medical Association, 175,* 1120-1128.

Osmont, K., & McFarlane, M. (1988). *What can I say?* Portland, OR: Nobility Press.

Osterweis, M., Soloman, E., & Green, M. (Eds.). (1984). *Bereavement: Reactions, consequences and care* (Report by the Committee for the Study of Health Consequences of the Stress of Bereavement, Institute of Medicine, National Academy of Sciences). Washington, DC: National Academy Press.

Palmer, E., & Watt, J. (1987). How to start a bereavement support group. *Living and working with bereavement* (pp. 121-126). Calgary, Alberta: Detselig Enterprises.

Parkes, C. (1980). Bereavement counseling: Does it work? *British Medical Journal, 281,* 3-6.

Parkes, C. M. (1972). *Bereavement: Studies of grief in adult life.* New York: International Universities Press.

Parkes, C. M., & Weiss, R. S. (1983). *Recovery from bereavement.* New York: Basic.

Pollock, G. N. (1961). Mourning and adaptation. *International Journal of Psychoanalysis, 43,* 341-361.

Rando, T. A. (1985). Bereaved parents: Particular difficulties, unique factors, and treatment issues. *Social Work, 26,* 19-23.

Rando, T. A. (1992, October). *Acute grief and mourning.* Paper presented at the Widowed Persons Service National Conference, San Antonio, TX.

Ritter, M. (1989, May 12). Study focuses on reaction to widowhood. *The News,* p. B1. Stuart, FL.

Ross, C. E., & Duff, R. S. (1978). Quality of outpatient pediatric care: The influence of physicians' background, socialization and work/information environment on performance. *Journal of Health and Social Behavior, 19,* pp. 348-360.

Rossa, S. (1993, October). *Creating and facilitating a grief support group for older widowers.* Paper presented at a meeting of the Widowed Persons Service, San Diego, CA.

Rubin, M., & Rubin, M. (1992, October). *Support groups.* Paper presented at the meeting of the Widowed Person Service, San Antonio, TX.

Sanders, C. M. (1979-1980). A comparison of adult bereavement in the death of a spouse, child, and parent. *Omega, 10,* 303-322.

Sanders, C. M. (1989). *Grief: The mourning after.* New York: John Wiley and Sons.

Sarri, R. C., & Galinsky, M. J. (1967). A conceptual framework for group development. In R. D. Vinter (Ed.), *Readings in group work practice* (pp. 72-94). Ann Arbor, MI: Campus.

Schiff, H. S. (1986). *Living through mourning: Finding comfort and hope when a loved one has died.* New York: Viking.

Segal, S., Fletcher, M. & Meekison, W. G. (1986). Survey of Bereaved Parents. *Canadian Medical Association Journal, 134,* 38-42.

Seiden, O. J., & Timmons, M. J. (1984). *Coping with miscarriage.* Blue Ridge Summit, PA: Tab.

Selye, H. (1976). Philosophic implications. *The stress of life* (rev. ed., pp. 427-456). New York: McGraw Hill.

Sewell, C., & Brown, P. B. (1990). *Customers for life.* New York: Pocket.

Shuchter, S. R. (1986). *Adjusting to the death of a spouse.* San Francisco: Jossey-Bass.

Silverman, P. R., MacKenzie, D., Pettipas, M., & Wilson, E. (Eds.). (1974). *Helping each other in widowhood.* New York: Health Services.

Silverman, P. R. (1981). *Helping women cope with grief.* Beverly Hills: Sage.

Silverman, P. R. (1987). The impact of parental death on college-age women. *Psychiatric Clinics of North America, 10,* 387-404.

Slagle, K. W. (1983, October). There is no grief like the loss of a ... *New Woman,* pp. 53-70.

Spangler, J. D. (Ed.). (1988). *Bereavement support groups: Leadership manual* (3rd ed.) (pp. 68-69). Denver, CO: Grief Education Institute.

Staudacher, C. (1987). *Beyond grief.* Oakland, CA: New Harbinger.

Stearns, A. K. (1984). *Living through personal crisis.* Chicago, IL: Thomas More.

Stephens, S. (1972). *Death comes home.* New York: Morehouse-Burlow.

Stoddard, S. (1978). *The hospice movement: A better way of caring for the dying* (pp. 1-14). New York: Vintage Books.

Stroebe, W., & Stroebe, M. S. (1987). *Bereavement and health.* New York: Cambridge University Press.

Susser, M. (1981). Widowhood: A situational life stress or a stressful life event? *American Journal of Public Health, 71,* 793-795.

Sweeney, D. R. (1991). Professional solutions. *Overcoming insomnia* (pp. 220-242). New York: Bantam.

Tatelbaum, J. (1989). *You don't have to suffer.* New York: Harper and Row.

Tavris, C. (1982). *Anger: The misunderstood emotion.* New York: Touchstone.

Tedeschi, R., & Hamilton, K. (1991, winter). Support group experiences of bereaved fathers. *Thanatos,* pp. 25-28.

Thomas, L. (1980). Dying as failure. *The Annals: The Social Meaning of Death, 447,* 1-4.

Toder, F. (1986). *When your child is gone: Learning to live again.* Sacramento, CA: Capital.

Traub, M. (1990, February 10). Women fare better than men when spouse dies. *The Tribune,* p. B1. Fort Pierce, FL.

Vachon, M. L. S. (1980). A controlled study of self-help intervention for widows. *American Journal of Psychiatry, 137,* 1380-1384.

Videka-Sherman, L. (1982). Effects of participants in a self-help group for bereaved parents: Compassionate friends. *Prevention in Human Services, 1,* 69-77.

Van Ornum, W., & Mordock, J. B. (1990). Death. *Crisis counseling with children and adolescents* (pp. 68-85). New York: Continuum.

Vineyard, S. (1990). *The Great Trainer's Guide.* Downers Grove, IL: Heritage Arts Publishing.

Walsh, J. A., & Ruez, J. F. (1987, July/August). Murder in the workplace. *EAP Digest,* pp. 34-37, 67-69.

Walterman, F. (1984). Publicity/public relations and public service. *Post Conference Report of the Widowed Persons Service Seventh National Conference, October,* 19-22.

Westberg, G. (1973). *Good grief.* Philadelphia: Fortress.

Whipple, D. L. (1992, January). *Bereavement groups: Topics and techniques.* Paper presented at the meeting of Florida Hospices, Inc., Ocala, FL.

Widowed Person's Week—an idea for your community. (1987). *WPS Insights, 29,* p. 3.

Williams, R. M. (1988, July/August). The wave of self-help. *Foundation News,* pp. 28-32.

Wolfelt, A. D. (1987, summer). Understanding common patterns of avoiding grief. *Thanatos,* pp. 2-5.

Wolfelt, A. D. (1988). *Death and grief: A guide for clergy.* Muncie, IN: Accelerated Development.

Wolfelt, A. D. (1988, October). *Five reconciliation needs of mourning.* Paper presented at the Widowed Persons Service National Conference, San Francisco, CA.

Wolfelt, A. D. (1989, winter). Empathetic understanding. *Thanatos,* pp. 11-13.

Wolfelt, A. D. (1990). Gender roles and grief: Why men's grief is naturally complicated. *Thanatos, 15*(3), 20-24.

Wolfelt, A. D. (1993). *Helping yourself heal during the holiday season.* Batesville Management Services.

Worden, W. J. (1986). Grief. *Post Conference Report of the Widowed Persons Service Ninth National Conference,* 2-4.

Worden, W. J. (1987, October). *Identifying complicated bereavement.* Paper presented at the Widowed Persons Service National Conference, Arlington, VA.

Worden, W. J. (1988, October). *Groups.* Paper presented at the meeting of the Widowed Person Service, San Francisco, CA.

Worden, W. J. (1991). *Grief counseling and grief therapy: A handbook for the mental health practioner* (rev. ed.). New York: Springer.

Worden, W. J. (1993, October). *When grief goes wrong.* Paper presented at the Widowed Persons Service National Conference, San Diego, CA.

Yalom, I. D. (1985). *Theory and practice of group psychotherapy* (rev. ed.). New York: Basic.

Index

Made in the USA
San Bernardino, CA
03 February 2017